CONTENTS

In spite of his long association with man the horse is far less domesticated than pets such as dogs; survival instincts remain strongly developed, and his delicate digestive system, which has evolved over millions of years, does not adapt well to the artificial conditions in which he is kept. Horses were not designed for riding, yet we expect them to submit to unnatural, stressful activities and are surprised when physical or psychological problems crop up.

For a horse to perform and behave well he needs to be physically and mentally contented, relaxed, and comfortable in his surroundings and work. When devising a daily care routine it is best to try to keep him in as natural an environment as possible; and when he has to be stabled you should try to alleviate stress and boredom.

Handling and riding must be correct and show an understanding not just of physical requirements and abilities, but of equine psychology. A horse's actions can at first seem baffling and incomprehensible to a newcomer, but they will often make more sense when they are examined with a measure of common sense and an appreciation of the horse's inherited survival traits.

A good owner will therefore make a point of learning as much as possible about the physical and psychological characteristics of horses, both in order to avoid creating problems and to be able to enjoy a truly harmonious partnership. A well-known dog training expert once commented that there were 'no bad dogs . . . only bad owners'. The same comment can also be applied to an extent to horses and ponies, although more often it might perhaps be fairer to say that many problems arise not so much because of 'bad' owners but simply inexperienced ones. With so much literature on horse and pony management and riding now widely available, there is no excuse for ignorance, but putting theory into practice can sometimes be another matter altogether, particularly when dealing with an animal which seems dauntingly big and strong. This is frequently when trouble starts. Anyone contemplating taking on their own horse or pony would therefore be well advised to try to obtain some firsthand practical experience before taking the plunge.

Of course, not all problems are of the owner's making; they may be the result of previous thoughtless, ignorant or even intentionally cruel handling by another person. While some cases may be irredeemable, others will respond gradually to careful, understanding management; with extreme problems, however, it is essential to realize your own abilities and limitations and when necessary to seek expert advice. Never be either embarrassed or too proud to ask for help from someone more experienced if you need it.

CROWOOD EQUESTRIAN GUIDES

Curing Bad Habits

KAREN BUSH

First published in 1994 by
The Crowood Press Ltd
Ramsbury, Marlborough
Wiltshire SN8 2HR

British Library Cataloguing-in-Publication Data

A catalogue record for this book is available from the British Library.

ISBN 1 85223 788 0

Picture credits

All photographs by Karen Bush
Line-drawings by Claire Colvin

Throughout this book, 'he', 'him' and 'his' have been used as
neutral pronouns and refer to both males and females.

Typeset by Dorwyn Ltd, Rowlands Castle, Hants.
Printed and bound in Great Britain by BPC Hazell Books Ltd
A member of The British Printing Company Ltd

Chewing is a destructive habit, expensive when items need to be repaired or replaced, and could lead ultimately to more serious habits (such as crib-biting), which, once acquired are almost impossible to cure. In youngsters chewing may be due to teething as much as curiosity, although in the case of wood-chewing, it may stem from imitation of another horse, extreme hunger, or possibly a dietary deficiency of some kind.

Teething trouble can be relieved to an extent by asking your vet for a soothing preparation to rub on the gums. Boredom is a factor to be considered if a horse is kept stabled for any length of time; turning him out in the field is really the best solution, and will do much to prevent other stable vices from arising.

If it is essential to keep the horse stabled, leave him with a hay-net to pick at; greedy types who make short work of a hay ration (or if only a limited amount is allowed) can be slowed down by using a net with small holes (such as those used for hay-lages), by placing one net inside another, or even by suspending it so that it swings freely and is more difficult to eat quickly. Stabling the horse where he can see activity going on in the yard will also help to relieve boredom.

Discourage chewing by painting wooden and projecting surfaces with a proprietary, unpleasant-tasting substance available for the purpose. Lead ropes which are chewed can be replaced by a length of chain with a spring clip at each end. Do not leave grooming kit or saddlery lying around within reach as it offers temptation – leather especially seems to be irresistible to horses!

> **Boredom**
> Turning a horse out in the field with other equine company is the best way of preventing boredom, although this is not always possible. Besides supplying a hay-net when the horse does have to be stabled, hang up a large swede by drilling a hole through the centre and threading a piece of knotted rope through it; hung so that it can swing freely, it will provide some amusement as the horse tries to nibble it.

Protect wooden surfaces from being chewed by covering them with an unpleasant-tasting substance. A proprietary wood-protector can be used on exterior surfaces such as fencing.

Biting – or nipping – can be common amongst entire male horses and ponies, being one of the ways in which they exert their authority over herd members and rivals. Very dominant equines of either sex may also exhibit this behaviour – it is not confined to stallions alone.

There can be other reasons for biting too, including nervousness, jealousy, self-defence and downright aggression; whatever the reason, it is not a habit to be treated lightly or tolerated, and a reprimand must be given instantly. The cause of it, however, may need to be taken into account when dealing with the horse in the future. The problem can often arise as a result of provocation: for example a mare with a new foal can be expected to be defensive and protective of her offspring, and will 'warn off' unwelcome intruders with teeth and, if necessary, heels.

A nervous horse, or one that has been ill-treated, may also be inclined to bite and in such cases erasing the habit will depend as much, if not more, on the handler's gaining the horse's trust and confidence as on reprimanding him. Some horses may be inclined to nip during certain activities although otherwise are good to handle – objecting to being groomed or having a girth tightened perhaps. Horses that are very ticklish need to be handled with a little tact, using soft brushes, a soft cloth or even just a hand to clean the most sensitive areas; girths should be tightened gradually, not yanked up abruptly or so that the soft skin behind the elbow is pinched. If you cause the horse discomfort, you really cannot blame him for attempting to retaliate in kind – there is a limit to how much even the most placid of animals can put up with. Youngsters can also be prone to nipping, and it is wise to discourage this early on before it becomes a more serious matter.

HANDLING KNOWN BITERS

With a horse known to be inclined to nip or bite when being handled, it is a good idea to tie him up short so he cannot reach the person dealing with him; this should not be seen as a way of restraining the horse whilst continuing to cause him unnecessary discomfort, otherwise he may well resort to using his feet in lieu of his teeth. It is also a sensible precaution to wear a padded jacket of some kind which will offer more protection. Try to avoid working in the stable or fussing over the horse when he is eating, as your presence can make him feel threatened and act aggressively.

Safety

Known biters kept in yards where inexperienced people and children are present, should be moved to a secluded area where possible, and a warning notice placed outside the door. It is also wise to fit a full metal grid over the top half of the door as an added precaution.

When a horse does bite (or threatens to), punishment must be instantaneous: say 'No!' firmly and smack him sharply on the neck – never the head or muzzle as this could make him headshy. There are some horses whose tendency to use their teeth goes beyond the occasional nip: with those who actually lunge towards the handler with open jaws and a threatening expression a tougher line may be necessary. A horse that acts in this way is unsuitable for an inexperienced person to handle, not least because any nervousness and lack of confidence will quickly be picked up and lead to a worsening of the situation. The handler should stay alert, and if the horse lunges at him in this fashion a sharp smack on the end of the nose with a short stick may be entirely justified. Having made the point, do not continue to punish the horse, as this only makes him more defensive, resulting in resentment of, and aggression towards, humans; eventually a problem animal may even become a savage one.

Irritability
Biting or nipping is just one of the symptoms of irritability; to an extent this can be avoided by sensible and fair handling – and by remembering that while some horses thrive on fuss and attention, others loathe it. Consistency in behaviour is vital; if possible a regular daily routine should be established – variations in feed times for example, may lead not just to problems such as colic, but also to signs of ill temper. Not surprisingly, physical pain can also be a key factor in causing irritability, and in some cases it may be useful to ask a vet to examine the horse for possible problems.

Indiscriminate feeding of titbits is also inadvisable, since the horse comes to expect them as a matter of course; he becomes irritable if they are not forthcoming, and may attempt to bully the handler into producing more treats. Praise or a pat is often a more suitable form of reward. Although it is sometimes necessary to resort to bribery, try to avoid making a habit of it if possible, and always bear in mind that offering titbits to a horse in full view of others can soon produce jealous and aggressive behaviour amongst those left out.

Known kickers should always be treated with caution since, although with correct and sensible handling they may improve, it is unlikely that they will ever be completely cured of the habit.

Kicking is often a defensive action which a horse will employ to protect or rid himself of something he sees as a threat. Even with a horse that is not prone to kicking it is inadvisable to approach him directly from behind without some kind of warning of your presence, and he should certainly never be greeted with a hearty slap on the quarters which may startle him into an instinctive defence reaction. Treating him in a manner which causes pain or discomfort is also very likely to make him kick out and so should be avoided.

If you have to deal with a horse that kicks, encourage him to approach you head first; if necessary, offer a titbit. Once he is facing you, immediately put on a headcollar; and whilst grooming or carrying out other chores, tie him up or ask someone to hold his head so he is unable to pin you against a wall or corner and kick. If

Using Headcollars

Although putting on a headcollar over the stable door is not usually to be recommended, it may prove to be the safest policy when dealing with extreme cases – or even leaving the headcollar on all the time, making it easier to catch hold of the horse before he can swing his quarters round.

When leaving a headcollar on, ensure that there are no fittings or fixtures on which it can become snagged (including water and feed bucket handles). Doorbolts can also be a potential hazard, but using a fully enclosed 'pony-proof' bolt will solve the problem. The headcollar should be a snug fit so that a hoof cannot become trapped in it, but check that it does not chafe.

Taking hold of the tail just beneath the end of the bone and applying a downwards pressure will have an inhibiting effect on a horse that kicks.

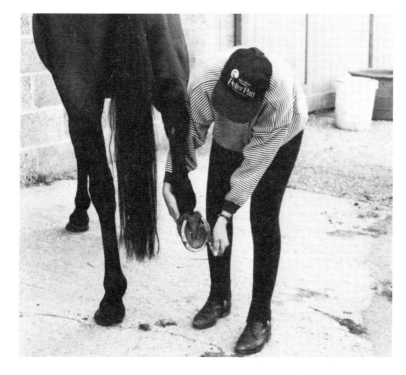

Always pick up back feet correctly, with your arm passing inside the limb, not behind it, and staying fairly close so that if the worst happens you do not receive the full force of a kick.

necessary, an assistant can hold up one forefoot to help limit the range and severity of a kick.

When grooming the quarters, always stand a little to one side of them; but stay fairly close so that rather than receiving the full force of a kick you will be pushed away. Using a free hand to apply a firm downwards pressure on the tail just beneath the bone can have an inhibiting effect, and if the horse does try to kick you will get some advance warning, as it is usually preceded by a violent swish of the tail.

When reprimanding a horse for kicking, a sharp 'No!' and smack on the neck or shoulder is the best line to take; a smack on the quarters or flanks might seem more appropriate but is actually more likely to lead to his kicking out again in retaliation. Correction may be necessary, but do not forget that this habit is often caused in the first place by poor handling or bad treatment, resulting in a distrust and dislike of humans generally, so try not to be excessive or over-zealous in punishment.

Horses that habitually kick others when turned out in the field should be put in a paddock on their own.

Kicking in Company
Horses that kick when in company should have a red ribbon plaited into the top tail hairs as a warning to other riders, particularly when attending shows or out hunting when there is a tendency to gather in groups. If you have to, take the horse off to a safe distance and keep him walking forwards to reduce the danger. If out riding with friends, keep a horse known to kick at the rear where it cannot do any damage – remember that serious injury can result not only to other horses but to riders as well.

Basic Precautions

Always wear sensible clothing when leading, including solid footwear (preferably with steel toecaps), gloves and a hard hat. While a bridle provides more control than a headcollar, it may not be ideal for a youngster not yet ready for a bit, and a lunge cavesson or a 'controller' halter may be better.

Do not try to lead by holding the bridle or headcollar noseband since fingers can become trapped if the horse pulls away. With fractious horses, ensure that all gates leading on to public roads are shut before leading him out of the stable.

Ideally, horses and ponies should be taught to lead properly while still young; as foals they can be encouraged to follow mum, being led with a soft cloth round the neck. Later this can be replaced with a foalslip or soft headcollar, and the foal gradually persuaded to walk alongside and eventually at a short distance from her. He should never be coerced or pulled forwards, as this will only make him panic, struggle and attempt to pull free; if necessary, an arm can be placed behind the quarters to push him forwards and this should be sufficient to overcome any initial reluctance.

Later in life difficulties may be experienced with mature animals which either hang back at every step or alternatively try to charge forwards and break free – often because early lessons have not been correctly taught, or through stubbornness, wilfulness or disobedience.

Horses that hang back and refuse to walk out freely are not only irritating but place the handler at risk of injury. Trodden-on heels are painful; while if the horse rears, the handler is in an extremely vulnerable position and will find it difficult to exert any real control. Try to remain between eye and shoulder, give a brisk command to 'Walk on!' and begin to walk forward; if the horse lags behind give him a tap with a short stick behind your back, on his girth. Repeat this each time he starts to lag behind; as some horses may take exception to the stick, lead in a bridle rather than a headcollar. If he tries to swing sideways away from the stick, teach the lesson alongside a wall, hedge or fence (although not a barbed wire fence), to keep him straight. Horses that tend to wander sideways towards

A whip may be used to give the horse a tap on the girth region to teach him to walk forwards more freely. The fence helps to keep the horse straight while doing this.

the handler can be discouraged by using a hand, or the stick handle, on the shoulder to push them away.

Horses that attempt to rush off and break free can be a problem, especially if they are large and strong and the handler is weak and inexperienced. It is vital to remain alert; using a bridle will provide more control than a headcollar, and by keeping the horse's head turned slightly towards you and bracing your right elbow into the neck muscles, it is usually possible to prevent the horse from getting the upper hand. With very strong, determined horses it may be necessary to enlist the help of someone else (preferably reasonably strong as well as experienced). Put on a lunge cavesson as well as the bridle and walk with one person on each side, one leading from the bridle, and the other from the lunge cavesson.

Using a Leadrope
When leading from a headcollar or bridle, hold the lead rope or reins at a distance of 10–15cm (4–6in) from the end, keeping your right hand behind the horse's lower jaw so that he is unable to take a nip at you, as well as to give you more control. Never wrap a lead rope round your hand; if you need more grip, tie a knot in the end instead. Keep the spare length of lead rope coiled neatly in your left hand where it will not dangle in the way, tripping up you or your horse.

Use a bridle with strong horses, and if necessary brace an elbow against the neck.

If leading problems only occur on specific occasions – as when entering or leaving a stable or trailer – it might be a result of more than just bad manners or training; there may be genuine fear or claustrophobia at the root of it. Very fit or overfresh horses, or those kept stabled for long periods, may also be more troublesome when being led.

Even if your horse is normally well behaved and sensible, never leave him tied up and unattended; nine times out of ten he will probably be fine, but you can guarantee that on the one occasion when you are not around something will spook him. If he then jumps backwards in surprise or alarm, the feeling of restraint and being unable to retreat any further than the end of the lead rope may cause him to panic further until eventually something breaks – the rope, headcollar, or possibly his neck. At best he will be loose; more seriously he may sustain severe damage to the musculature or vertebrae of the neck. Whatever the outcome, it is likely that in the future he will be difficult to tie up, either because he has had a frightening experience, or because he has learnt how to free himself whenever he wishes.

If he does show any signs of anxiety or hanging back, attempting to tug him forwards again will only make matters worse; slacken the tension on the lead rope and push him forwards with a hand on the

Never tie a horse directly to a fixed object, but to a piece of twine that will break in an emergency.

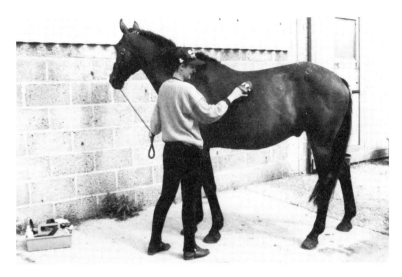

Do not tie up difficult horses, but loop the lead rope through a ring on the wall, keeping the free end in one hand.

quarters instead. If he is nervous, soothe him with your voice until he is relaxed before retying him. Try attaching a small hay-net to a separate ring for him to nibble at while he is tied up to discourage hanging back.

When teaching a youngster or retraining a difficult horse to be tied up, it is best initially to attach a long rope or lunge line to the headcollar, looping it through a ring on the wall so it slides freely, and keeping hold of the spare end in one hand. If he begins to pull backwards, play out the line so there is no direct pressure to alarm him and make him struggle more. Lead or push him forwards again, taking up the slack, and giving the command 'Stand'.

Four Basic Rules

1. Never tie up a horse using the reins of his bridle – if he pulls back it may damage his mouth.
2. Always use a quick-release knot.
3. Tie up to a piece of breakable string, never directly to a fixed object. Alternatively use an 'Equisafe Tie Ring' which incorporates a break-away device; these rings should not, however, be used for hanging hay-nets from.
4. Do not feed your horse while he is tied up, as in order to reach the feed bucket you will need to give him a lot of slack in the lead rope, over which he may catch a forefoot if he paws at the ground.

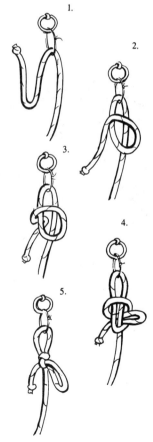

Quick-release knot.

Correct position of handler to horse when lungeing.

Bad organization of lungeing equipment will not only lead to problems, but can be extremely dangerous. In this picture the handler has the rein looped tightly round her hand, so is likely to be pulled over if the horse tries to run away, and the lunge rein is trailing on the ground where either horse or handler could become entangled with it.

Lungeing can be a tremendously useful exercise when correctly managed; however, problems can crop up for various reasons – not all of them the horse's fault! Frequently problems arise because the horse does not understand what is required of him, or as a result of physical difficulties, or through bad handling of the equipment or loss of initiative by the handler. Lungeing can also be a very strenuous and demanding exercise for the horse, and an over-tired horse will soon become evasive and resistant to further work. For this reason, lungeing sessions should be limited to fifteen or twenty minutes' duration.

IGNORING COMMANDS

This is usually a result of lack of understanding. Return to basics, leading the horse and giving commands to halt, walk and trot, suiting the actions to the words, and he will soon begin to connect them. At this point, ask an assistant to lead the horse on a large circle while you give the commands; as the horse begins to respond to your vocal commands, the assistant can begin to move away from him towards the centre of the circle, and eventually can be dispensed with altogether.

It is vital that the commands are always consistent – use the same words in the same tone of voice each time, or he will never really understand. A short, sharp command with an upwards inflection is most effective when asking for upwards transitions, with a soothing, lower-pitched voice with long drawn out syllables for downwards transitions, for example 'Tr-OT!' or 'W-a-a-a-lk'.

The handler is better organized here, although the horse is finding it hard to cope with the small size of the circle.

NOT GOING FORWARD

This problem can arise if the side reins are too short and the horse is unable to move forward freely; over-shortening them can also make the horse feel so restricted that he rears. Some horses can, however, become very idle on the lunge once they know they are out of range of the whip, although the possibility of physical problems should not be ruled out and a vet consulted if felt appropriate.

Shortening the lunge rein and walking on a small circle so as to be positioned a little closer to the horse usually solves the problem if the horse is just being idle; alternatively, enlist the aid of an assistant who can send the horse forward firmly from behind with a whip, walking on a smaller inner circle, while you remain at the centre holding the lunge rein and giving the commands.

REFUSING TO HALT

If the horse refuses to halt when asked, try spending some time leading him and asking him to halt frequently as before, giving a verbal command at the same time. If it happens while lungeing, circling the lunge rein gently in a backwards direction may help, but this should be discontinued if it upsets the horse; check also that the whip is held and used correctly in case its position or movements are alarming him.

Fences and hedges, provided they are imposing enough, can be used to help halt the horse if necessary. The handler will need to take care not to allow the horse to rush forwards past her, however, and will need to tuck the whip under her arm facing away from the horse before approaching, so he does not become frightened. Ideally brushing boots should be used on all four legs; if you only have one pair of boots, put them on those limbs most likely to be injured.

If this is unsuccessful, the horse can be directed towards the nearest·fence (*never* a barbed-wire one) or hedge and given the command to halt as he comes to face it; the handler will need to be positioned almost opposite the inside eye so the horse cannot dash past him. To do this successfully, the fence must be sufficiently high and imposing that the horse will not attempt to jump it.

TURNING IN

A horse that has been allowed to become bored with lunge work soon learns evasions, such as stopping and turning in towards the centre of the circle; this can also happen if he is very stiff and finds the work physically difficult. Having turned in, the handler is at a disadvantage, because the horse can either run backwards or swing round and move off in the opposite direction. If it happens, you must halt him, approach him, lead him back to the original circle and start work again, this time paying strict attention to your position in relation to the horse.

Stand opposite the inside hip, so as to be able to drive him forwards effectively; keep him moving with activity in all gaits and, if he is very stiff, perhaps make the circle a little larger so he can cope more easily. Standing opposite the inside eye or shoulder makes it difficult to keep the horse moving forwards and almost impossible to stop him swinging inwards if he feels like it. Having an assistant to send him forwards with the whip as described above can also be of help.

PULLING AWAY

A horse that tries to swing his quarters inwards and run out of the circle can also present real difficulties, particularly if he is strong. Lunge in a confined area, or a corner of the field, and if he does begin to try to hook off be prepared to act quickly: once he has got onto a straight line it will be extremely difficult to stop him, even if you are fairly strong. Drop the whip if necessary, place both hands on the lunge line, keep your knees bent and lean back on the line, using your dead weight and voice to bring him back to a halt; this will only succeed if your positioning is correct in the first place. If this fails, let go rather than be pulled over and dragged.

Rather than allowing the horse to realize that he is so much stronger than the handler, it may be wise in such circumstances to use a Wels pattern lunge cavesson, which fits like a drop noseband and will give more control, or alternatively to lunge directly from the bit. This can be done by attaching the line to the outside bit ring, running it over the top of the poll and threading it back through the inside bit ring, and passing it back to the handler. It must be appreciated that although this is effective, it can be very severe – changing the action of the bit to that of a gag – so it is important to seek advice before doing this.

Do make sure that the way in which the whip is handled is not at least partially to blame – do not flourish it but use it quietly, and never use it to punish. If the whip is used in such a way that the horse becomes frightened, he may well attempt to put some distance between himself and it.

EQUIPMENT

It is important to use the correct equipment, to ensure safety, control, and ease of handling. To work the horse correctly you will need the following:

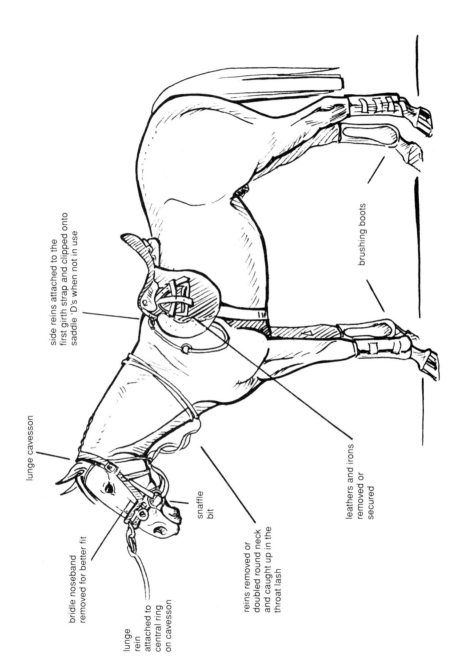

side reins attached to the first girth strap and clipped onto saddle 'D's when not in use

brushing boots

lunge caveson

leathers and irons removed or secured

bridle noseband removed for better fit

snaffle bit

lunge rein attached to central ring on caveson

reins removed or doubled round neck and caught up in the throat lash

Correct lungeing equipment.

Lunge Cavesson This should be a snug fit so that it does not move on the horse's head; a well-padded noseband will help to reduce the danger of chafing. The metal plate on the noseband should have two hinges for preference to ensure a better fit, and the central ring to which the lunge rein is normally fastened should swivel freely.

Lunge rein This may be made of webbing, cotton or nylon; nylon is very light and can be slippery to hold. It should be at least 6.5m (21ft) long, and the buckle or metal clip which attaches to the cavesson should be fitted on a swivel so that the rein does not become twisted.

Lunge Whip This should be fairly light but with a well-balanced stock, and a long thong about 2.5m (8ft) long with a lash on the end.

Brushing Boots If the horse is stiff, likely to misbehave, young, lacking in co-ordination or balance, he is more likely to injure himself on a circle, so brushing boots should be used on all four legs for protection.

Side Reins These may be plain, or with elastic or rubber inserts, according to personal preference. They should be easy to adjust and are normally fitted at the same height and length.

Saddle or Lunge Roller The side reins are attached to either the girth straps or the rings on the lunge roller; if a saddle is used, the stirrup irons should either be run up the leathers and secured, or removed altogether.

Bridle A simple snaffle bridle should be used, with the reins removed or doubled round the horse's neck, twisted round each other and caught through the throatlash. The lunge cavesson should be put on so that the noseband section passes beneath the cheekpieces – removing the bridle noseband will ensure a comfortable fit.

Young or Arthritic Horses

Make allowances for young horses who may find it difficult to balance on three legs for long periods; as they grow tired or begin to lose their balance they are likely to attempt to slam their feet back down or to kick out. Older horses suffering from arthritic conditions may also experience discomfort when the joints are flexed, as may those with back problems, so it is best not to insist that the feet are lifted higher than necessary. Pulling the hind legs out too far to the side can also cause discomfort and loss of balance. If a horse is likely to kick, wear a hard hat and gloves.

If a horse refuses to pick a foot up, stand close beside him, grasp the fetlock joint firmly and lean against the shoulder or flanks to displace his weight off it. Firmly pinching the area between cannon bone and tendons just above the fetlock joint will also help. Once the foot is off the ground, support the hoof and keep the joints well flexed; by continuing to lean slightly against him it will help discourage him from leaning his weight on you.

If a horse is inclined to kick out with a back foot the joints should also be kept flexed; at the same time take hold of the end of the tail in the hand supporting the hoof, so that a firm downwards tension is maintained. This trick can also be used with a horse that leans his weight on the handler – provided the tail is long enough, use the end to form a cradle for the hoof so that he is in effect holding himself up. Make sure that you support the hoof with your hand passing in front of the foot, not behind it, so as to minimize the risk of a dislocated shoulder, and never attempt to pick up both the feet from the same side.

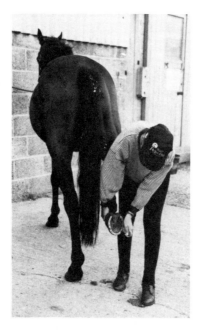

Picking up a hind foot incorrectly – compare this with the picture on page 9.

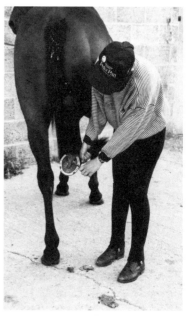

One way of preventing the horse from leaning his weight on the handler while picking out the back feet.

Farriers cannot be blamed for refusing to shoe a horse that is diffi-cult; often, however, the reason horses become like this is that they have had a bad experience in the past – such as a pricked sole, or rough, unsympathetic handling – which has caused pain or discom-fort. If the farrier then becomes impatient and abrupt because the horse is anxious and unco-operative, it is not really surprising that the whole process of shoeing degenerates into progressively worse battles. Unfortunately, not all farriers are sympathetic towards a horse's problems and fears, so if you do find one who is as good at handling horses as at shoeing them, it is worth keeping him even if he costs more or you have to travel to him. Difficult horses put a farrier at risk of injury (which is a serious matter if it means he is unable to work for a while), and take more time as well as patience to shoe, so you should be prepared to pay a little more for the service in such circumstances. Correct handling and appreciation of any physical problems should help; also spending time rebuilding confidence by tapping the feet with a light hammer, and stabling where other horses can be seen being shod, should improve mat-ters. With very difficult horses it may be advisable, at least initially, to sedate them; advice should be sought from your vet.

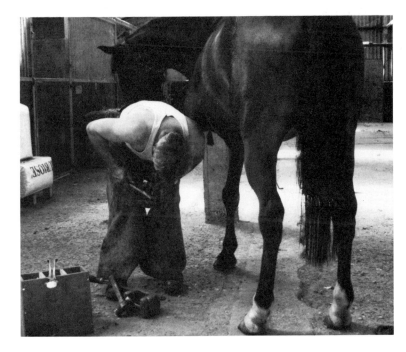

A farrier who is as good at handling horses as he is at shoeing them is worth cultivating.

Horses that are difficult to groom are usually only so because of thoughtlessness by the handler. Some horses are more sensitive than others, but most have ticklish spots, and repeated roughness will rapidly lead to signs of ill temper such as biting or kicking. Never use stiff-bristled brushes on tender areas and take care not to bang bony prominences with the sides of wooden- or plastic-backed brushes. Be especially patient with those horses that are ultra sensitive, using only soft-bristled brushes, or even just a soft cloth or fingers, to gently tease out clinging patches of dried mud or sweat, even though it will take a little longer.

Mane and tail pulling is painful for some horses, best tackled gradually over a period of time, removing only a few hairs as they are pulled out rather than large chunks. Major sessions will leave the horse feeling sore, inclined to rub, and likely to be even less co-operative the next time. Some horses object strongly when a comb is used, but are more amenable if hairs are pulled out with the fingers instead – a plastic washing-up glove or rubber thimbles will protect the finger tips.

When pulling a tail, the horse may try to kick out, so have someone hold him inside a stable with his tail to the door. Place a blanket over the door and drape the tail over the top while working on it to minimize the risk of injury.

Whiskers on the muzzle function to an extent as sensory organs, and if the horse really objects to their removal (a plastic safety razor is easiest and safest) it is kinder to leave them. Fidgeting while the feathers are trimmed can be easily dealt with by asking someone to lift the opposite leg.

Extremely Difficult Horses

With such horses it may be felt that the whole process of pulling the mane or tail is too traumatic to persist with; and a reasonably neat effect can be obtained using a razor comb bought from a chemist. Alternatively, the mane can be left long and for shows be put into one long, continuous running plait along the crest of the neck.

If a horse has to live out most or all of the time, it is kindest to leave the tail unpulled and allow the forelock to remain fairly long as protection against bad weather, and flies in summer. A neatly plaited tail looks just as good as a pulled one for smart occasions!

Use a soft cloth or sponge on sensitive areas such as around the eyes and muzzle.

In so many cases this problem could have been avoided with proper management; once a horse has become anxious it takes much time and patience to try to restore his confidence and trust.

Horses are easily startled by abrupt, unexpected movements and if these are repeatedly made around the head area he will quickly become wary. Punishing a horse by smacking him on the nose or hitting him round the head, using a badly fitting bridle which pinches the base of the ears, using an uncomfortable bit, or banging his teeth with the bit when the bridle is put on or taken off, can all cause him to become headshy. Physical problems such as toothache, or ear or sinus infections may also be a cause.

When handling the head, untie the horse in case he pulls backwards in alarm; use a soft cloth or fingers for cleaning, and avoid resorting to brute force as this will only reinforce any fears. Putting the bridle on may be difficult with extreme cases, and it may be necessary to take it apart and put it on in pieces.

With a headshy horse, take every opportunity to handle the head, gently stroking the neck and gradually working upwards as close to the head as possible. Use your voice to relax him, and possibly offer a titbit at the same time, both to distract him from what you are doing and to encourage him to lower his head.

Exercise great patience and tact with a horse that is headshy; when grooming him it may be necessary to use a soft pad or just fingers, rather than a brush.

Nothing looks worse than a rubbed mane or tail; even when it does grow back (which can take some time) it rarely looks quite as good again! Persistent rubbing may be caused by a number of things.

PARASITES

Hygiene
Lazy grooming and sloppy stable management can be to blame if dirt and scurf have been allowed to accumulate. The dock should also be cleaned each day with a damp sponge kept specifically for this purpose.

Tail rubbing can be induced by worms, and a regular worming programme should be observed throughout the year at six-to-eight-weekly intervals using an appropriate anthelmintic. Lice can also be a cause, and, as with worm infestation, it may be noticed that there is a corresponding loss of condition: the coat will appear dry, dull and lifeless, with the hairs tending to stand up, rather than being sleek and glossy. If you part the hairs and look at the roots, it is possible to see the eggs, which look very much like small hayseeds. The affected horse, and all others in contact with him, should be treated with a louse powder available from a vet or good saddler. Other parasites can cause itchiness too, and, if observed, you should consult your vet.

SWEET ITCH

This unpleasant form of skin irritation is caused by an allergic reaction to the bite of a particular species of midge. Affected animals

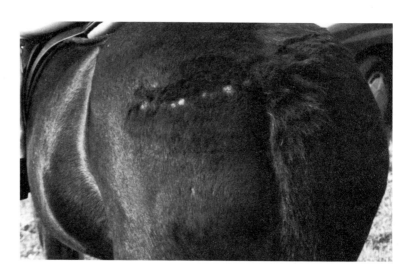

Sweet itch.

will frantically scratch the crest, withers and the base of the tail against any available surface, often until raw and bleeding. The symptoms appear during the spring months and may continue through to the late autumn; in severe cases veterinary treatment may be necessary. Good stable management is essential: use fly repellants, keep the mane and tail clean, rub special preparations into the skin, and stable the horse during those periods when the midge is most active.

> **Pulling**
> Pulling the mane and tail can also cause soreness and itching if too much is attempted in one session. It is best to tackle it gradually over a period of time; it will also be less uncomfortable for the horse if done when he is still warm after exercise.

TRAVELLING

Tails may be rubbed during travelling if the horse has a tendency to rest his quarters against the ramp or sides of the trailer or horse-box. This usually occurs because he is finding it hard to balance, so the driver may need to be more considerate, particularly when accelerating or negotiating corners – horses cannot anticipate such things. A tail bandage and tail guard provide some protection.

STANCE

Tails may appear to be rubbed if the horse is adopting an unusual stance – resting his quarters against a wall or manger in his stable, for example, which might be an indication that he is trying to relieve some kind of physical pain elsewhere. Veterinary advice should be sought.

BATHING

The horse's skin can be surprisingly sensitive to some products, even though they may be used with no ill effect by humans. For this reason it is best to use shampoo products that have been specifically formulated for use on equines, rather than cheaper substitutes such as washing-up liquid, which can be harsh on the skin and cause irritation. Many of these equine products also have an added bonus in that they are low lathering and mildly insecticidal.

It is important that after shampooing the mane and tail (or the body) all soap suds are thoroughly rinsed out; if allowed to dry into the hairs, the coat will not only be left looking dull and scurfy, but itchy too.

When bathing use products formulated especially for horses, and ensure that all the suds are thoroughly rinsed off.

Trace clip.

Blanket clip.

Hunter clip.

Chaser clip.

Sweat or 'bib' clip.

If a horse has had a bad experience in the past – such as being nicked – it is understandable if he is apprehensive and unco-operative about being clipped; but there are some who would appear to have no such excuse and are troublesome year after year. There can be contributory factors – fear of the cable, dislike of the noise or vibration – but even when these are minimized they can still be difficult. Before resorting to more extreme measures, there are several ploys which may be worth trying. Cotton wool placed in the ears will help muffle the sound; and it does sometimes help the horse to become accustomed to the noise if he can be placed in a stable near other horses being clipped.

Using lightweight clippers with a less powerful motor will often prove successful, as they are quieter and produce less vibration; the very small, rechargeable or battery-operated types normally used for clipping heads and trimming up may be tolerated better than those operated from an electric mains supply. The narrower blades will make it a longer job, and if a large area is to be clipped it may need to be completed over several sessions, but it can prove to be a way around the problem; and once confidence has been gained, it may even ultimately prove possible to use conventional heavy-duty clippers.

Another source of anxiety is the cable attached to the clippers; if the horse is likely to be difficult, a trailing cable which can be trodden on (or become entangled round the legs) can be something

Clipping Rules
1. Clip in a well-lit stable rather than outdoors.
2. Remove water buckets from the stable.
3. Make sure the blades are sharp – blunt ones not only clip poorly, but will pull painfully at the hairs.
4. Check that the clippers are properly earthed.
5. Do not attempt to clip a wet or sweaty horse.
6. Groom the horse thoroughly before starting – dirt and grease will clog up the blades, causing overheating and bluntness.
7. Adjust the tension of the clipper blades correctly, according to the manufacturer's instructions.
8. Tie long hair out of the way, and wear rubber-soled boots.
9. While clipping take care that the horse does not stand on the cable.

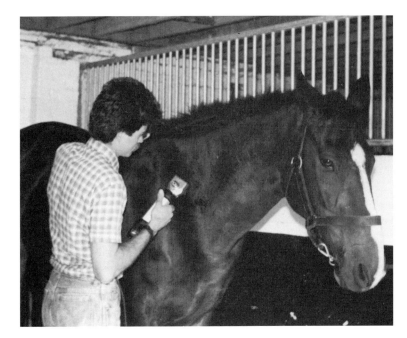

Be prepared to be patient and take more time with a horse that is anxious about being clipped.

of a safety risk to both animal and human. It is possible nowadays to buy clippers run off a portable rechargeable battery pack worn around the operator's waist, which does away altogether with the need for a long cable. Just as importantly, it enables the handler to move freely around the horse, reducing the time needed to complete the clip.

If you have the patience, and all else fails, most horses will tolerate hand clippers, although these are extremely tiring for the operator to use, and will generally only be practical for small areas – the neck and chest for example.

With awkward horses, when a more extensive clip is required, or for very ticklish areas, a twitch may be sufficient to restrain him (provided it is employed before he has had a chance to get worked up about it). With the really difficult cases, however, where attempting to clip could prove hazardous to either the horse or operator, sedation may be the only way of getting the job done. An intravenous injection given by a vet is by far the most satisfactory and successful method.

Twitch

Horses or ponies who push their handlers to one side when entering or exiting their stables are something of a liability. Not only is there a danger that the person who is leading them may be crushed against the door jamb, trodden on or knocked flying, but there is a very real risk that the horse himself may be seriously injured should he catch a hip against the door-frame, or succeed in breaking free.

It may be due to genuine fear or to downright bad manners, so when dealing with this problem, take into account the horse's previous history, his personality and any physical expressions of his state of mind.

All too often people are guilty of being less careful than they should be when leading through narrow entrances. Stable doors should always be constructed so as to open outwards, and should be fully opened before attempting to take the horse through them. On windy days take special care that doors do not blow back on the horse, trapping him or painfully banging a hip; this only needs to happen once to make the horse anxious and inclined to hurry through in a panic in case it occurs again.

Stable doorways should also be sufficiently wide; in purpose-built boxes they are likely to be fine, but in buildings which have been converted for use as stables they may not be satisfactory. A minimum width of 1.4m (4½ft), with a minimum height of 2.2m (7ft) is the ideal; bear in mind that if the lintel is too low the horse may catch his head.

It is important to lead a horse into the stable correctly, always walking through in a straight line, rather than at an angle, and positioned between eye and shoulder rather than at the shoulder. This allows control to be retained, with less danger of being pushed to the side by the shoulder itself – and allows more room for the horse to move through the doorway. Make sure the horse is fully in the stable before attempting to turn him around.

FEAR

With an anxious horse be firm but not abrupt, as shouting and rough handling will only make things worse. Be ready for him to rush, taking a firm hold on the lead rope or reins (a bridle may give more control) and use soothing commands, praising him when there are any signs of improvement. Some horses may panic more if they feel crowded by the handler when going through a doorway, regardless of how the handler deals with the situation, and will persist in

Safety First
Never walk in front of the horse as he goes through a doorway – if he does suddenly rush forward you will most likely be knocked over and trampled on. When leading a saddled horse through a doorway, ensure that stirrup irons are run up the leathers so they cannot swing around or become caught up on anything. Never attempt to ride a horse into or out of a stable.

rushing through. With a horse like this, it may be safer simply to lead the horse to the entrance, put the lead rope or reins over his neck out of the way, and allow him to progress through at his own rate. If the horse leaves his box in this fashion, a second person should be stationed outside to catch him as he emerges, and the yard itself should be enclosed.

BAD MANNERS

Bad manners is another cause of this habit, the horse exhibiting a lack of respect for his handler's authority by pushing him to one side and forcing his way past. Remedying this will rely on correct, rather than sloppy, handling at all times, and probably on teaching the horse to be more obedient and to lead properly in hand. When grooming or working around the horse generally, it is not a bad idea to insist that he moves across from you in response to the pressure of a hand and a command, as this will help to instil a sense of your dominance over him. Using a bridle or lunge cavesson will help, particularly with stronger horses; remain alert, and if the horse makes any attempt to dive forwards he should be checked firmly and reprimanded with your voice. Try to avoid leaving feeds or hay-nets ready in the stable but take them in once the horse is inside, as anticipation of food will make him even more anxious to enter the stable quickly.

Entering the Box
When opening a door, undo the bottom bolt before the top one so you do not risk getting knocked out, and insist that the horse moves back away from the entrance as you go in. Do not forget to close the door properly behind you again or you are asking for trouble! Horses that tend to push through a doorway the moment it starts to be opened can be foiled by fitting a breast bar inside at chest height; this can also make it easier to carry out routine stable chores.

Breast bar

When using this type of removable feed manger, which can be hooked over the top of a door or fence, check that it is at a suitable height, particularly for small ponies, who will otherwise find it difficult to eat comfortably.

'Bolting' feed – eating it too quickly – is not uncommon in stabled horses, and results in food being insufficiently chewed and mixed with saliva before swallowing. This can lead to choking, digestive disorders and unthriftiness.

Giving a small hay-net prior to a concentrate feed will help to take the edge off the horse's appetite; adding chaff will also help to encourage more thorough chewing. Large chunks of rock salt placed in the feed manger can also slow down eating to an extent. Check the daily stable routine to see if feeds can be made more frequent, though the size of each ration may need to be reduced in consequence. Allow the horse peace and quiet while eating; human presence can make him bolt his food because he feels threatened.

Reluctance to eat may be a result of illness, or physical problems such as sharp teeth, lampas or mouth ulcers, which will need veterinary attention. 'Quidding' – when the horse drops pieces of partially chewed food out of his mouth – is often a sign of mouth problems, and he may refuse to eat foodstuffs that require more chewing. Foodstuffs should always be of good quality – if past their best they will not tempt shy feeders – and changes or additions to the diet made slowly to allow the digestive system to adjust more easily, as well as giving the horse time to get used to them. Feed mangers should be kept clean, as encrusted stale food can produce an offensive smell. When on a high-concentrate intake, it is not uncommon for a horse to go off his feed. It is best then to reduce the ration until the appetite is regained, and perhaps to consult an equine nutritionist who may be able to devise a diet that is less bulky but provides the same energy value.

The Horse's Digestive System

Horses are 'trickle' feeders: their systems are designed to cope with a more or less continuous intake of low-grade nutrients with little variety, consisting of large quantities of bulky food with a high cellulose content. Domestication means that food is regulated into specific measured rations throughout the day, rather than being continuously available. Horses are most comfortable when their stomachs are half full, and five hours after a full feed they will be feeling hungry. Feeding little and often, and preferably at the same times each day, are therefore golden rules to follow in order to try to reach an acceptable compromise between the horse's needs and ours.

Shy feeders can also be tempted by adding sugar beet, diluted molasses, cooked linseed or stout to feeds. Carrots, apples, turnips, swedes or mangolds can also be added, but should be sliced into fingers rather than chunks so they do not cause choking – or else coarsely grated and mixed in.

BED-EATING

Some horses are particularly greedy and, when kept on straw and left to their own devices, will persist in eating large quantities of bedding. It is worth remembering that, in his natural state, a horse would normally spend a large percentage of the day grazing; depriving him of this activity by keeping him stabled for long periods, particularly if he is on a reduced hay ration, will soon make him bored and hungry as a result of a lack of bulk in the diet. If the hay ration is poor quality, the horse may be eating his bedding simply because clean straw seems a more attractive option.

It is definitely a habit to be discouraged, however, as it can lead to digestive problems such as colic, and aggravate respiratory diseases; it also removes the handler's control over food intake – which can be important if the horse is on a diet to remedy obesity, or if he needs to be lean and fit for fast work. If large quantities of bedding are eaten, it could also leave insufficient covering on the floor to protect him from injuries if he lies down.

Discouraging bed-eating

1. Ensure a minimum hay ration of 25 per cent of the total daily food intake.
2. Split hay rations into two or three, and use hay-nets with small holes to make it last longer and keep the horse occupied.
3. Provide a swede suspended on a rope for the horse to nibble at when his hay has gone.
4. Use only good-quality hay.
5. When adding fresh straw to the bed, mix the new in thoroughly with the old to make it less palatable.
6. Sprinkle a weak solution of disinfectant and water over the surface of the bed to make it less tasty.
7. Try to turn the horse out as much as possible.
8. If necessary, change to a different bedding such as woodchips, shredded paper, peat, or rubber flooring.

Slice apples and root vegetables into fingers, not chuncks, to minimize the danger of choking, before adding to feeds to tempt fussy eaters; alternatively they may be grated.

Coprophagia

Horses that eat their own droppings may do so through boredom, extreme hunger or a dietary deficiency. On the whole it is not a desirable habit since it results in worm reinfestation; when young foals do this, it is a means of building up gut bacteria. If horses have had such bacteria depleted through the use of antibiotics they may also exhibit this habit. Droppings should be frequently removed from the stable, sufficient hay provided, time in the field allowed, and a mineral and vitamin lick supplied. If, after taking these measures, things do not improve, seek veterinary advice.

Boredom, lack of activity, insufficient exercise, stress and lack of forage can all be contributory factors to these vices, which are behavioural problems purely associated with stabled horses and are never observed in wild horses. Once a horse has learnt how to crib-bite or windsuck, it is virtually impossible to prevent him doing it, even though the environment, diet and management may all be changed.

CRIB-BITING

Chewing or crib-biting may possibly be a response to the genetically programmed urge to graze, and grasping projections with the front teeth imitates biting off grass stems, while swallowing air distends the stomach as grazed forage would normally do.

A crib-biter will grasp any available projection with his front teeth and, arching his neck, will swallow air, making a peculiar and unpleasant grunting, gulping sound as he does so. The resulting accumulation of air in the stomach can lead to digestive disorders, and horses with this vice can be poor doers. It can also lead to recurrent attacks of colic. Horses that crib-bite will often show un-even wear of the incisor (front) teeth.

Prevention is the best remedy, since there is no 'cure' as such; care should be taken never to leave the horse standing in the stable for long periods with nothing to occupy his attention. As much as possible, he should be turned out, preferably with other horses or ponies for company, and when stabling is necessary, he should be provided with a hay-net. Stabling which overlooks the yard is ideal, as being able to watch activities going on helps provide some additional stimulation and alleviate boredom.

A hay-net will give a horse something to occupy his attention and satisfy his urge to graze when he is in his stable.

Crib-biting often develops from a tendency to chew protruding wooden objects in the stable, such as projecting struts and the tops of doors, although feed mangers and other fittings may also come in for attention. A nutritional deficiency can be an underlying cause in the case of a horse that habitually chews wooden structures, so a balanced diet should be provided. The number of chewable surfaces should be reduced to a minimum: cover door tops with a metal strip to minimize damage, and give feeds in buckets which can be removed when not in use, rather than use permanently fixed mangers. Any structures showing signs of chewing should be painted with an unpleasant-tasting substance to nip such tendencies in the bud early on.

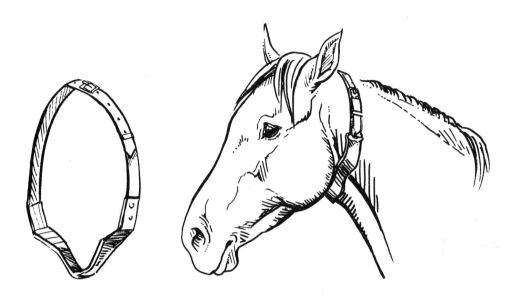

These measures can also be taken with a confirmed crib-biter; also turning him out to graze may help to distract him temporarily, although the habit is likely to return back in the stable. Some horses will continue to crib-bite even so, using fences and gates. Surgical operations have been used to prevent this vice, but their success is variable; the easiest and most effective method of correction is to use a crib strap. This is a leather strap with a shaped metal section, which is buckled around the top of the neck and physically prevents the horse from being able to swallow air when his neck is arched.

Crib strap.

WINDSUCKING

Windsucking is a progression from crib-biting; the horse still arches his neck and swallows air, making the same characteristic noise, but can do so without needing to grasp a projecting surface with his teeth. Deal with the problem in the same way as crib-biting.

Both crib-biting and windsucking, if severe, can result in the muscles on the underside of the neck becoming larger, as they contract when the horse arches his neck to swallow in air. This is unsightly, and can also make achieving a correct headcarriage difficult when riding. This habit consitutes unsoundness and, when selling a horse on, it should be declared at the time of sale.

A horse that 'box-walks' is one who is unhappy in his environment – perhaps being confined in the stable for overlong periods with insufficient exercise, or maybe being kept next to another horse with whom he does not get along. Some horses simply find being kept stabled intolerable, in which case they are probably better off being kept out at grass as much as possible. This should preferably be with other compatible equine company; there is no doubt that even if a horse can be turned out for only a few hours it does a great deal to help him unwind and relax mentally.

Yard routines should also be examined. Depending on the horse's personality, he may find it less stressful to be stabled in a quieter part of the yard, where there is less disturbing bustle; others may actually do better if they can see the activity going on outside; if boredom is suspected to be a part of the cause this can prove to be a successful solution. Daily routines should be as regular as possible, otherwise more highly strung animals can become irritated and distressed. It should go without saying, of course, that whoever rides and cares for the horse on a regular daily basis, should be fair in their treatment of him.

Some people advocate putting bales of straw in the way or hanging tyres from the ceiling to prevent box-walking, but all these measures do is make it more difficult; they will not actually stop it, and could prove to be hazardous. Since the bedding will inevitably become disturbed and bare patches of floor may be exposed, it may be advisable to put down rubber flooring which will protect the horse from injury if he settles enough at some point to lie down. Leaving him tied up is unfair, denying him mobility and doing nothing to deal with the cause of the problem – his state of mind.

Hanging up a swede on a rope can provide amusement for stabled horses.

Turning your horse out whenever possible, especially with other equine company, will do much to improve his state of mind.

There are many more horses who suffer from claustrophobia – a fear of being confined in an enclosed space – than is realized, and it can often be at the root of a number of other problems, ranging from being difficult to lead into stables, to being virtually impossible to load or travel in a trailer or horse-box. Horses who suffer from this problem will show unmistakable signs of fear and panic: wide, staring eyes, muscles tensed and ready for flight, ears laid back, and possibly breaking out in a patchy sweat. Even if the horse is persuaded to enter, he may continue to panic, throwing himself around, and possibly injuring himself in the process. He may even try to escape confinement in a stable by attempting to climb or jump over the bottom door.

As with people, there are different degrees of claustrophobia, and with those who are only mildly affected it may be possible to stable them for short periods – overnight for example – provided they are handled tactfully and with sensitivity so as not to increase their fears. When this is possible, stables should be large and airy, with a high ceiling and a view to the outside; when leading the horse in, it often helps to switch the interior light on so as to make the stable seem less forbidding.

Horses that are more badly affected may refuse to enter a stable at all, even when considerable physical duress is applied. If you have a horse this bad, it is unfair to try to force him; horses are unable to rationalize and come to terms with their fears as humans can, and trying to push the issue will only increase his sense of panic, and is not far short of mental cruelty. It is perfectly possible to keep most horses out at grass all year round if necessary, provided adequate shelter, food and rugs are supplied. Sometimes it may be possible to reach a compromise of sorts if a large barn is available, or an open yard with a three-sided shelter.

Patience, reassurance and sometimes the offer of food may encourage the horse to enter the stable (particularly if the handler has established a good balance between trust and obedience). No attempt should be made to force or rush him as this will lead to increased resistance from the horse. With difficult cases, if stabling is essential for some reason, it may be possible to use a blindfold, although this should not be done with young horses, only those that are mature and unlikely to become headshy. It must be put on quietly to avoid frightening him, and he may need to be walked in a couple of circles to disorientate him before approaching the stable. Have someone walking beside the horse with a hand on his quarters to help guide him straight through the doorway and talk in a soothing voice.

If allowed to persist, this habit can prove highly irritating and disturbing for both neighbouring horses and humans living nearby, as well as damaging the door and frame, and possibly injuring the horse; it can lead to bruised and enlarged knee and fetlock joints and jarred feet.

It is frequently an expression of frustration which can be due to a number of reasons. As discussed elsewhere, it is not a natural state of affairs for a horse to be kept in close confinement for long periods, and every effort should be made to turn him out at grass each day for as long as possible, so that he can graze, move around freely, socialize with other horses and generally relax mentally. When it is necessary for him to be stabled, a hay-net should be available and perhaps some other form of amusement offered, such as a swede suspended from a rope. It is also important that the horse receives sufficient exercise.

Door-kicking can also be a demand for attention. If the horse is more inclined to kick the door at specific times – such as when feeding – ensure that he is fed first, rather than made to wait, which will not teach him to be better behaved, but only make him more irritable.

Having started to kick at the door, some horses will continue to do so, purely from habit and enjoyment of the sound. It can help to break the habit (provided an effort has been made to remedy the initial cause) if the door is left open and a breast bar fitted instead so there is nothing to kick at. During the daytime in fine weather this may be the most satisfactory solution, although, since the bottom door will have to be shut at some point – at night perhaps, or if it is rainy – its interior should also be padded in some fashion to minimize the danger of injury and effectively to muffle the noise made.

Breast bar fitted to prevent door-kicking.

Rather than remedying the cause, many people are often content simply to deal with the symptoms of problems such as this – by closing the top door of the stable or fitting a full metal grille for example – so that the horse cannot get close enough to the door to be able to kick with his front legs. It is not a particularly satisfactory solution since, although the particular problem is stopped, it is only a temporary solution and the horse is likely to take refuge in some other, perhaps even less agreeable, habit; or to resort to kicking at the back walls with his hind feet instead.

A horse that consistently knocks over his water bucket risks not only standing on a sodden bed, but not having water available when he is thirsty – neither of which is particularly desirable. Check that buckets are not situated in a position where they are most likely to get tipped over – next to the doorway for example – and that it is something the horse is doing intentionally, through boredom.

If necessary, buckets can be placed in a metal bracket attached to the wall, or in an old tyre placed in a corner of the stable. Alternatively a heavier container can be used; very large plastic buckets can be bought which hold the equivalent of two and a half normal-sized buckets of water, or even use a plastic dustbin. The quantity of the water, as well as the size of the container, will ensure that it cannot be knocked over. More expensively, an automatic watering system can be fitted, although some horses will play with them and succeed in soaking a considerable portion of bedding.

Feed buckets may also be kicked over, often through impatience, resulting in a percentage of the food becoming trampled into the ground and wasted. A portable manger hung over the top of the bottom door may provide an answer, or alternatively fitting a fixed manger to the stable which cannot be dislodged.

Types of Bucket
If buckets are used, either for food or water, they should be made of rubber or plastic rather than metal, which could lead to injury, particularly if the horse is inclined to kick them over. Handles should also be removed so that feet cannot become caught in them.

Metal bucket holder

Plastic dustbin

Bucket inside rubber tyre

Large 2 bucket-size container

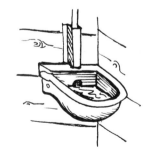

Automatic waterer

Alternative ways of providing water in the stable for horses that kick over buckets.

'Weaving' is the term applied to a horse who stands in his stable, rocking from side to side, the head and neck swinging; in some cases the movement is quite violent, with the weight shifting from one front foot to the other. A horse who weaves constantly is in danger of injuring his front legs and wearing his front shoes excessively, and may also be a poor doer.

PREVENTION

It is usually a sign of boredom or anxiety, and is more frequently seen in horses that are of a highly strung and nervous disposition. Some horses will be seen to weave only at certain times, such as feed times, which assume a greater importance for a horse kept stabled for most of the time, than for one that is out at grass for all or part of the day. A regular daily stable routine, and provision of a hay-net when stabled, as well as sufficient exercise and liberty, is therefore vital in preventing this habit from starting.

The horse's own individual temperament should also be taken into account: try to stable him in the location he is going to be happiest in. Some prefer a view across the yard where they can see everything that is going on, which helps to prevent them from becoming bored. More temperamental and easily excited horses may do better in a quieter place where there are fewer disturbances and unexpected noises to upset or startle them. Whoever rides the horse must also be prepared to shoulder some responsibility for the horse's frame of mind in the stable. Making demands he cannot meet or adopting bullying tactics will only make him progressively more anxious, no matter what efforts are made to settle him in the stable.

With a horse that is caught weaving during the early stages, it may, with good management, be possible to prevent it from becoming an established habit. Once it has become established, however, it will always be reverted to at times of stress and anxiety, even though appropriate measures may be taken and some improvement noted.

Most horses weave with their heads over the stable door; this can be inhibited by mounting a metal grid with a V section cut out in the centre, by cutting out an oval section in the top door and then closing it, or by fixing an upright piece of wood to the lower door. Another solution is to suspend an old tyre from the top of the doorway so that if the horse does attempt to weave, it swings back

Weaving grid.

and gently bumps him on the side of the head. This also has the merit of providing a plaything for younger horses, but it will have to be fastened to the side, out of the way, when the horse is entering or leaving the stable.

Using devices such as this allows the horse to continue to look out over his stable door, while preventing him from being able to weave. The only drawback is that, finding himself unable to weave, he may simply withdraw from the doorway and continue to do so at the back of the stable; hence the importance of adopting other measures as mentioned above to improve his quality of life.

Keeping the lead rope out of sight, offer a titbit as an incentive to be caught. Leaving a headcollar on is a sensible idea when a horse is known to be awkward; this one has a fly fringe fitted.

Difficulty in catching is probably one of the commonest problems amongst horse owners; and those who have experienced it will no doubt agree that it is also one of the most frustrating and time-consuming. Sometimes the blame can be laid at the owner's door – if the horse is only caught up to be ridden, it does not take long for him to become wise to this, and start to be evasive of capture; even if he is always given a titbit or small feed on such occasions.

This is not always strictly the case however: some horses are never any trouble at all to catch no matter how they are treated, while others are difficult for no apparent reason, and this can be one of the most irritating aspects of the problem. While there are several ruses which can be used to catch a horse on an immediate basis, it is unwise to rely on them as a permanent solution as success may not be guaranteed every time. It is certainly worth taking a more far-sighted view and thinking about whether a change in the daily routine and care of the horse might not achieve more satisfactory long-term results. The following points might also be considered with a horse that is normally easy to catch, to prevent him from ultimately becoming difficult!

1. Vary the time you ride each day, otherwise the horse may become wary about being caught at these times.
2. Make a point of visiting several times a day when the horse is out, and catching him up without riding, offering a small titbit if necessary, so that he begins to welcome and look forward to your arrival, rather than dreading it.
3. Always handle the horse correctly and fairly, otherwise he will soon learn to keep his distance.
4. Keep work within the horse's capacity, providing variety and some activities which he enjoys.
5. Do not use the fact that a horse is difficult to catch as an excuse for not turning him out at all, as this is only likely to lead to other problems.
6. However difficult a horse has been to catch, always praise and reward him when you finally succeed. While you may feel more like telling him off, it will do nothing to make him more co-operative in the future!

SHORT-TERM TACTICS

1. Leaving a headcollar on the horse will make it easier to catch

hold of him. Be patient when trying to take hold of the horse however; a sudden lunge towards the headcollar is likely to result in the horse leaping backwards abruptly. As he does this he may successfully pull free of your grasp (and will be very reluctant to come near you again) or, if you manage to keep hold, could drag you after him, resulting in injury. Leaving a short length of stout rope attached to the bottom ring of the headcollar can be useful, since it is easier to take hold of without startling the horse, particularly if he is also headshy.

2. Greed will often get the better of some horses, eventually overcoming their desire not to be caught. A handful of nuts or a favourite titbit may be enough to tempt them, or even rustling a piece of paper. Others may respond better to a few nuts being rattled in the bottom of a bucket, associating the sight and sound with feed times. Do not chase after the horse with the food, but rather advance as close as possible, and then patiently bide your time, rattling the feed bucket to gain his interest and encourage him to approach you. With crafty types who will stretch their heads right out and snatch a few nuts from your palm while keeping as much distance as possible, a bucket is usually more successful, since he has to get closer and put his nose right in to reach the food at the bottom. If possible, hold the bucket by your side so you can quietly take hold of the headcollar from the side – grabbing at it from the front will startle the horse into pulling backwards.

3. If the horse is kept out with others, bringing them in will sometimes do the trick, although this can be time-consuming; once he realizes he is on his own, he may be more inclined to be caught.

4. With enough people to help, a very difficult horse may be cornered by forming a line and gradually herding him into a secluded part of the field. This is not always an ideal method, as it requires plenty of people, and some horses may panic when they realize what is happening. This can result in his trying to jump or climb over field fencing when he finds himself trapped, or trying to barge through the human line, so it is not something to be attempted by children. Caution is advisable when approaching a horse that has been successfully cornered using this method, as he may try to kick out; be patient, use a soothing voice and offer a titbit to encourage him to approach you.

5. When fewer people are available, form a human line with each person taking hold of the end of a lunge line to form a moving

Using Headcollars
Minimize the risk that is involved in leaving a headcollar on by making sure it is a close fit so that it cannot become dislodged, and nothing can become caught up through it – although it should not be so tight it causes rubbing. Checks should be made each day to ensure that it is not chafing; if signs of soreness become apparent, pad the offending areas well with sheepskin and adjust the fit if required. Light-weight leather headcollars are preferable to the nylon variety which may not break in an emergency. They will, of course, need to be well cared for, being regularly cleaned, soaped and when needed, oiled, in order to keep them comfortable and supple.

Offering a few nuts or titbits to another horse in the field will sometimes provoke jealousy in the one that does not want to be caught, so that he then decides to push in and get his share. Do take care if trying this – and also when walking into a field carrying a feed bucket when other horses are present: if a fight over the food breaks out, the handler will be left in a vulnerable position in the midst of flying hooves and teeth.

Walking down a horse, not allowing him to stop and graze, works with some horses, but does require fitness and plenty of time. Be careful not to get in the line of fire of the back feet.

barrier. The same dangers are present, with the additional hazard that if the horse tries to run through or jump the lunge line, he may become entangled with it and brought down.

6. Many horses become difficult to catch in the spring, when better weather brings an improvement in the quantity and quality of grazing, so they are less reliant on supplementary feeding. Spring grass is often more tempting than titbits which aggravates the problem. After a few weeks, matters may settle down and the horse will once again become easy to catch, but if not, moving him to a sparser paddock may be the best solution, although he should receive adequate food for his needs by supplying hay if necessary.

7. Some horses may treat it all as a game, allowing the handler to approach to a certain distance each time before moving off, or even circling around just out of reach. Patience and food may be the best solution, but it is sometimes worth experimenting with a different approach. Rather than adopting a passive approach, keep walking after him, not allowing him to stop to graze so much as a mouthful, but offering a titbit or a feed bucket as an incentive to give himself up. Do not attempt to chase or run after him, as it will be interpreted as threatening behaviour, or may excite him and make him even less inclined to be caught. This can take some time, and does require a certain amount of fitness, but can be surprisingly successful if you have the patience. Over successive occasions, it takes progressively less time to catch the horse until it becomes comparatively easy.

Some horses may buck or kick out when they are first put out –
particularly if they do not normally get much time at grass, or if they
are fresh. Other horses may do so with a definite intent to injure;
and metal-shod hooves can cause tremendous damage if you are on
the receiving end of them.

Problems can also be caused by failing to open a gate wide
enough, so that the horse catches his hips as he goes through, or by
sloppy practices such as releasing the horse and giving it a slap on
the quarters with a hand. This can cause them to try to rush through
gateways or charge off immediately they are in the field. With fractious horses who have acquired this habit, it is a wise precaution to
take them out in a bridle, which will give more control, and, if they
are really difficult, to have another person on hand to open the gate
for you.

Having led the horse into the field, turn his head back to the gate,
which must be left slightly ajar so that you can easily slip back out
without becoming trapped. Now the horse has first got to turn
around before he can buck or kick out at you, during which time
you will have ample opportunity to make your escape. Spend a
moment or two before letting him go, patting and talking to him and
perhaps offering a titbit, to discourage him from spinning round
rapidly and behaving in such a manner.

Whether bringing in or turning
out, always make sure that gates
are opened wide enough and
not allowed to swing back on
the horse.

Groups of horses develop their own social hierarchy, and when introducing a new member, a certain amount of pushing, shoving, nipping and squealing will inevitably go on until the pecking order has been established. The group will usually settle down if left to their own devices without much harm being done; leading a newcomer around the field perimeter before turning the other horses out will at least familiarize him with the boundaries so he is less likely to become cornered or run into the fence. Leave a headcollar on and keep an eye on the group for a while in case things become more serious, and a quick rescue necessary.

In winter, put out more piles of hay in the field than the number of horses, placing them at a distance from each other, to minimize the risk of a dominant animal chasing off others to get more than his fair share. Always give concentrate feeds individually, not in a field where other horses are loose, to guarantee a correct ration.

Occasionally one particular horse may be picked on mercilessly, resulting in severe injuries. If this happens, the horse should be moved to another field with more gentle company, or the aggressor isolated. This sort of problem is more likely to occur when paddock space is limited; an individual who feels crowded may release his pent-up territorial aggression on newcomers who are considered to be intruders.

Groups of horses soon establish their own 'pecking order' but individuals who persistently bully others to the point where injuries arise are best isolated.

Whether a horse is an adept escape artist or not, all possible precautions should be taken to stop him from straying, when he may cause injury to himself or others. Fences should be checked every day without fail, and immediate action taken to secure any gaps or weak areas. Even if they are not necessarily big enough to accommodate the horse, it does not take a determined individual long to enlarge gaps sufficiently by pushing through them.

The fencing should also be suitable for the occupants of the field; sufficiently high enough to discourage jumping out, and with the gaps between strands of wire or rails small enough to prevent the animals from stepping through, rolling or crawling beneath them.

Damage to fencing can occur through horses leaning on it to graze verges on the other side, or by using uprights as scratching posts, thus weakening them. Horses can be prevented from browsing through fences by using properly secured close-mesh fencing. They can be discouraged from leaning on, or trying to break through fencing, by using electric fence tape, which can be bought by the metre and fixed to the top or inside. This is easily visible and most horses have a healthy respect for it if first led up to it and their noses pressed against it so they receive a shock.

Security Marking
There are several companies nowadays offering security marking for horses and ponies; whether kept stabled or at grass, marking is a good deterrent against theft as well as making it easier to trace owners of stray animals. Options open to owners include freeze-marking, a form of permanent branding using super-chilled markers, inserting microchips or hoof branding.

Freeze-marking is one method of security marking which acts both as a deterrent against theft and makes it easier for owners of strayed animals to be traced.

Saddlery should always be a good fit, suitable for the horse and correctly adjusted; yet it is surprising just how many owners neglect these very obvious (and very important) points when dealing with a 'problem' horse. They are so often at the root of problems, ranging from bit evasions to bucking, as well as causing a horse to become difficult to tack up. When buying new or secondhand saddlery it is best to obtain professional advice on its fit. Saddles are likely to be the most expensive single item of equipment you will purchase, and you should spend your money on one which does the job as well as possible, ensuring comfort and safety for both horse and rider.

Horses may also become awkward to tack up if there is some kind of physical discomfort present (such as galls, sores, deep-seated bruising, mouth problems) and it can be helpful to ask a vet to check the horse over thoroughly; some physical problems or injuries are only apparent to an expert. Some horses become awkward and unco-operative if they have been roughly handled – or even if they find work so unpleasant that they try to avoid being tacked up, to escape the exercise which inevitably follows.

SADDLE

Before putting the saddle on, put a headcollar on the horse and tie him up, to prevent him from wandering around, or nipping. If a numnah or saddle cloth is used, put this on first, positioned well forward towards the withers. Gently place the saddle on top, pull the numnah or saddle cloth up into the front arch and gullet of the saddle so it cannot press upon the spine, and keeping hold of both, slide them back into position so that the hairs are kept flat and the saddle rests in the dip of muscle just behind the withers. Gently lower the girth, checking that it is not twisted and without banging the knees with the buckles, and fasten it sufficiently firmly to hold the saddle in place until you are ready to mount. Never pull it up abruptly, and avoid using excessively wide or narrow girths which may cut into the skin, chafe or pinch. Always run up the stirrups before saddling up or unsaddling. When removing the saddle, again take care not to bang the knees or spine with the girth. If the horse is downright difficult about the saddle being put on, it may well be due to some kind of physical problem, and until this (and the saddle itself) has been checked, he should not be ridden. If apprehension and awkwardness is the cause, due to past injury or bad treatment, patience and reassurance are the best answers.

Checking the Saddle

Bear in mind that horses will often change shape during the year, depending on their routine, fitness and exercise, which may affect the fit of the saddle. Panels stuffed with flock will also settle with use, and may need to have more added periodically; occasionally the flock may form hard knots – usually if sweat has soaked through the lining – which can cause uncomfortable pressure points. A six-monthly check by a saddler is a wise investment against such problems arising.

Always place the saddle gently on the horse's back, sliding it back into the correct position so the hairs lie straight beneath. Check that the numnah is pulled up into the front arch and gullet so it does not press on the spine.

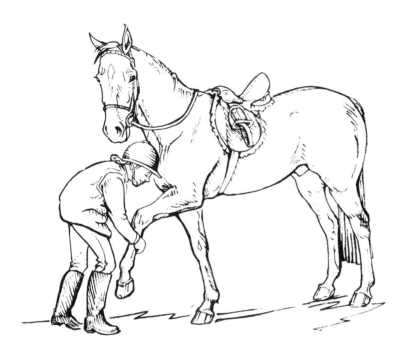

Stretch each foreleg forward after tightening the girth to prevent pinching of the skin behind the elbow.

With a difficult horse he is best tacked up inside a stable where his movements will be confined to some extent, and there is less danger of his trying to make a break for freedom.

BRIDLE

The most successful method, particularly with large horses prone to poking their noses in the air out of reach, is to place the right arm around the horse's nose, holding the bridle cheekpieces in the right hand, whilst offering the bit with the left hand. If necessary, the headpiece of the bridle can be used to capture the end of the nose and draw it down, until it is possible for the handler to place the right arm around the nose and prevent it from being raised again. If the horse refuses to open his mouth to accept the bit, slide a thumb into the corner of the mouth, where there are no teeth, and press down on the tongue. Offering a titbit, or smearing the bit mouthpiece with honey, treacle or a little minty toothpaste will often make this a more pleasurable experience. Horses frequently become difficult about being bridled up because they have repeatedly had their teeth banged, so do try to avoid this. With a horse who refuses to open his mouth and let go of the bit, offering a titbit again usually does the trick.

This is probably the easiest method of bridling up, as the handler can prevent the horse from raising his head up out of reach.

Once rug-tearing has become a habit it is extremely difficult to stop, and it may become necessary to use a clothing bib. This is a broad flap fitted beneath the lower jaw, which prevents the horse from being able to catch hold of stable clothing with his teeth, yet allows him to eat and drink normally. However, it is far better to try to prevent the habit from arising in the first place if possible!

Making Rugs Fit
Rubbed areas are a sign that a rug does not fit properly. Taking a tuck along the sides of the neck line and adding a gusset of extra material will allow freer movement of the shoulders, reducing chafing in this area, as well as helping to prevent the rug from slipping backwards, which can cause rubbing. Where breast fastenings are low, it frequently helps to move them to a higher position. If the withers are very prominent it may also be necessary to stitch in a block of thick foam rubber on either side to help lift the rug up, and form a channel similar to that of a saddle in order to prevent chafing.

Clothing bib.

Quite often there is a very good reason why rugs are torn; in the case of youngsters it may be due to the unfamiliarity, perhaps combined with teething problems. Introduce the concept of wearing a rug gradually over a period of time rather than waiting until you really need it.

Rugs should fit correctly so that they do not pinch or rub. Linings should be brushed daily to remove loose hairs and bedding, as these can make the horse feel itchy and try to remove the source of the irritation. With the advent of modern synthetic materials, washing rugs is made considerably easier, but it is worth bearing in mind that some horses may be allergic to certain biological soap powders or fabric softeners, which may cause itching.

Being too hot can also cause a horse to try to remove his stable clothing; rather than putting on all the rugs during the early evening when it is still sometimes quite warm, it is better to pay a late night visit when the temperature has dropped and add extra coverings then. Rugs should also be straight; if they hang crookedly, or are pulled forward into position against the natural lie of the coat, they can cause considerable discomfort. Where rugs have a tendency to slip, using crossing surcingles beneath the belly or a fillet string, and adding some judicial tucks and gussets to give a better shape, will often help keep everything in place.

Brush rug linings daily to remove loose hairs and bedding which may cause irritation.

New Zealand rugs which become torn out in the field often suffer less from direct damage by the horse than from barbed wire fencing. Snags from the barbs can be common in the chest area if the horse tries to reach over the strands of of wire to graze grass on the other side; small tears rapidly become larger ones, especially if they allow the rug to become dislodged a little and the horse worries at them. This can be prevented to an extent by asking a saddler to stitch in large patches of heavy duty rip-stop nylon, or even patches of leather.

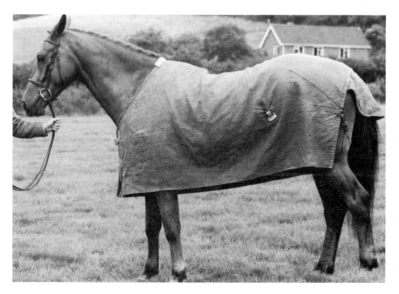

Buy the best-fitting rug you can afford. This New Zealand is nicely cut and shaped, particularly around the shoulders (leaving plenty of room for movement) and quarters, and has a choice of heights for the chest fastening. The depth of rug and tail flap help to keep cold gusts of wind away from areas often clipped in winter. If necessary you can always ask a saddler to modify an existing rug, adding gussets and taking tucks to improve the fit.

With cold-backed horses, it is especially important to tighten the girth gradually.

The term 'cold backed' refers to the behaviour of the horse when the saddle is placed on his back and/or girthed up; in mild cases he may either arch or hollow his back and appear to shrink from contact with it; in more extreme cases he may plunge and buck violently, sink or throw himself to the ground. It is highly unlikely that it is due to the cold touch of leather on his back (most people in any case use a numnah nowadays) but to a number of other causes listed below.

1.   Poorly fitting saddle.
2.   Back injury.
3.   Previous fracture of a rib or the sternum (breastbone).
4.   Soreness of back muscles – perhaps due to excessive work, a rider who is too heavy or has bad posture.
5.   Over-tightened girth.
6.   Galls or saddle sores.
7.   Apprehension of pain due to any of the above having occurred in the past.

Since many back injuries and deep-seated bruising can be virtually invisible to the eye, a vet should be asked to examine the horse thoroughly, as well as getting an experienced person to check on the fit of the saddle. Advice on this matter can be sought from staff of retail outlets who have had training in this respect, or from saddlers displaying trade badges (such as that of the Society of Master Saddlers). Qualified riding instructors may also be able to offer suggestions about the suitability or otherwise of fit. Other problems which are seemingly unrelated may in fact prove to stem from the same source, so it is important to investigate this aspect; until the cause has been identified, the horse should not be ridden.

If your vet does advise you to continue working the horse, some appear to benefit from being loosely girthed up and walked out in hand for ten minutes or so before tightening the girth more securely and mounting – preferably from a mounting block as this puts less strain on both horse and saddle. Using a fleecy numnah or 'jelly' pad may also help, as well as using a conventional girth rather than an elasticated one, which often tends to be done up more tightly.

In the case of a horse that behaves normally until the moment the rider attempts to mount, and then displays 'cold back' symptoms, in addition to those points already listed, the manner of mounting should be examined and an effort made to improve this skill if necessary.

Mounting (and dismounting) is something often very badly done by many riders, who are otherwise careful and conscientious about all other aspects of their horse's training and management. Not surprisingly, sloppy mounting ultimately causes awkward, unco-operative behaviour, with the horse refusing to stand still, or nipping; and strangely enough, this frequently seems to be tolerated by riders.

Getting on a very large horse can present problems for those who are short, and inevitably puts more strain on the horse's back and the saddle, especially if the stirrup has to be let down considerably. In this instance, using a mounting block is probably best for all concerned, and also with young horses, or those who are weak in their backs; one can be either made or purchased, or else a beer crate, bale of hay or straw used for the purpose. Avoid using unstable objects, however, for they can frighten the horse if they fall over.

Teaching the horse to stand still when being mounted (provided poor mounting technique, discomfort from saddlery or physical problems are ruled out) is largely a matter of training and patience, but well worth spending the time on. Make as though to mount, repeating the command to 'stand' or 'halt' (it helps if this has already been taught to the horse previously) at the same time. Each time the horse fidgets or tries to move off, insist that he stands still and start again, praising him when he does stand quietly. An assistant to hold the horse can be helpful initially, although they should be careful not to restrict the horse with the reins, as this can cause running back or even rearing.

Causes of Discomfort
Sometimes a horse will be awkward about being mounted because he is in pain, perhaps from some kind of back injury or girth galls, because the saddle fits badly, or because he is feeling sore and tender in the back muscles – caused by unaccustomed hard work, or an unbalanced rider. Another source of discomfort leading to nipping and fidgetiness is a girth which pinches the skin behind the forelegs; stretching the forelegs forwards after tightening the girth and before mounting often helps. The girth should also be a suitable width and not too wide, narrow, or over-tightened.

Never mount near a fence or in a stable, as this increases the risk of injury to the rider should the horse misbehave.

Be as athletic as possible when mounting: an assistant to hold the opposite stirrup will help to prevent the saddle slipping.

Using a mounting block is not just for the elderly! They can save a lot of unnecessary strain on both the horse's back and saddle.

Giving a leg-up.

Swinging a leg over the horse's head when dismounting is also dangerous; it can frighten the horse, and if it suddenly lifts its head very high or spooks at something, the rider can be knocked off and seriously injured.

Points to remember when mounting

1. Be as athletic as possible.
2. Settle lightly and quietly into the saddle; continually crashing down on to the horse's back causes discomfort.
3. With a horse that nips, have the opposite rein a little shorter so he looks slightly away from you. The reins should be short enough to prevent the horse moving forwards but not so short that he moves backwards in discomfort.
4. Take a handful of mane with the reins in the left hand for support, rather than the front of the saddle, and as you spring up reach for the waist, rather than the cantle. This will minimize the danger of the saddle being pulled to one side (which is uncomfortable for the horse), injury to the back muscles, or twisting of the saddle tree.
5. Ask the horse to stand up squarely before attempting to mount, so he is well balanced.
6. Check that the girth is tight enough before mounting so that the saddle does not slip; with very round-barrelled horses, ask someone to hold the opposite stirrup.
7. Avoid sticking a toe into the horse's sides, or kicking the quarters through not swinging the leg sufficiently high over the saddle and his back.

Horses will often enjoy a good roll when turned out in the field, and it serves a practical purpose as well as being a pleasant way to relieve an itch. Rolling helps to cool him down and make him feel more comfortable when he is warm and sweaty, whilst in the winter a layer of mud is acquired which helps provide insulation against the cold.

A horse which attempts to roll while being ridden, however, can cause damage to both the saddle and to his back, which can be injured by the saddle tree if he rolls right over. More seriously still, the rider can be badly hurt if he becomes trapped beneath the horse's bulk.

A few individuals will persist in this habit, having discovered that it is a good method of removing the rider, but these are fortunately in the minority; in most cases it tends to be a 'one-off' occasion, which, if it is repeated, tends to be in specific circumstances when the rider can at least anticipate it and take steps to prevent a repeat performance. Horses are most likely to roll when feeling hot and sweaty, when going through or standing in water, or when finding themselves on an inviting-looking patch of soft going. The first in-dication of the horse's intent is a lowering of his head while he paws with a front foot. This is followed by the front legs folding at the knees as the horse starts to go down. If the rider is quick-witted enough to keep the head up and ride strongly forward the attempt can usually be thwarted. A determined effort may need to be made, using not just the legs and voice, but the whip as well if necessary.

Once the front end has gone down, it is usually too late to do much about it, and the rider should quickly kick both feet free of the stirrups and jump off out of the way. If it is safe to do so, keep hold of the reins to prevent the horse's legs getting entangled in them, and use them as soon as possible to raise the head (if this is drawn upwards the rest of the body usually follows) to get the horse on his feet. If a horse does succeed in rolling on his saddle, his back and the saddle should both be checked for damage by a vet and a saddler respectively.

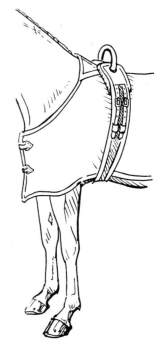

Anti-cast roller.

Rolling in the Stable
Horses that roll in the stable may run the risk of becoming cast – wedged against a stable wall with the legs trapped so they are unable to rise to their feet again – so it is advisable to use an anti-cast roller. This has a hoop-shaped piece of metal above the spine which prevents the horse from being able to roll right over.

'Bolting' is a term loosely applied to horses who become very strong and difficult to stop, as well as those who are genuine 'bolters'. The latter will gallop out of control and in a blind panic to the point of taking no notice whatsoever of either the rider or obstacles in their way. They are almost impossible to cure, and a horse who repeatedly bolts is a danger to everyone and best retired from work or destroyed, so there is no danger of his passing into the hands of a less competent rider.

Horses who take a strong hold as opposed to being genuine bolters can be just as frightening to ride, and just as dangerous, although in the right hands it may be possible to remedy the problem. Many horses will become over-excited and strong when ridden in company, particularly if cantering or galloping. The more obedient and well-schooled the horse is, the less of a problem this will be; even though he may still get strong, it will be possible to curb him. It is also worth trying to spend time on steady, disciplined schooling with other horses occasionally. Certainly, if it is suspected that a horse will get out of hand, fast work should not be attempted until he is more obedient and more submissive to the rider's wishes.

Avoid always cantering or galloping in the same places – or always when finding a grassy stretch or open area – as this will often cause the horse to anticipate it, and to become even more headstrong and difficult. When in company, it is also wise to place more gassy types at the front of the group; never allow the pace to get out of hand or push the horse on, and if someone does get into difficulties, do not pursue them out of a misplaced desire to help. There is nothing useful you can do to assist in such a situation, and it is only likely to make matters worse if anything – far better to follow on at a steady pace instead.

Some horses will become very strong in certain circumstances, such as when riding cross country, and a change to a stronger bit for such activities may be advisable. Not only will it give the rider more control, but is also ultimately kinder to the horse's mouth, saving it from much bruising and soreness.

EMERGENCY ACTION

If a horse does get out of control, it is vital for the rider to keep the upper body vertical, or even behind the vertical, with the heels deep and lower leg forward.

Heading for a hedge or fence in the hope that it may cause the horse to slow up or stop is not a good idea, as the horse may attempt to jump it or crash straight through it. Rather than applying a continuous pull on both reins, which the horse will only set its jaw and lean against, take sharp checks on both reins either at the same time or alternately; sometimes a sawing movement is most successful. It may not be classical riding, but at such moments looking pretty is not the most important of priorities! Keeping the hands high rather than low will be more effective. Should the horse try to drop his nose very low, dragging the rider forwards into a weak and ineffective position, bracing one hand on the neck while checking with the opposite rein will help.

Bolting – an effective position is vital!

Slowing Down
Bringing the horse on to a large circle if there is enough space will help to steady the horse; as the pace begins to slow the circle can gradually be decreased in size until control is eventually re-established. Attempting to bring the horse on to too small a circle too rapidly, however, could result in his becoming unbalanced and falling over. Always exercise care and make sure there is plenty of room available for such a manoeuvre.

Bucking can arise because of physical pain, and it may be wise to ask a vet to examine thoroughly a horse with such tendencies.

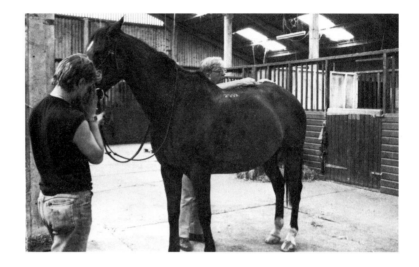

BUCKING

Some horses may buck through freshness, exuberance, excessive feeding or high spirits, but this habit can also be due to discomfort from saddlery or the work he is asked to do, physical pain, or from a definite desire to get rid of the rider.

A horse who has learnt that bucking is an effective way of removing the rider is likely to persist until firm steps are taken to suppress it. Anticipation, a secure position and quick reactions are important; in order to buck effectively the horse has to slow down,

Bucking.

and lower his head. If, at the first warning signs, the rider drives the horse positively forwards into a firm contact with the hands raised, it may be possible to nip a potential buck in the bud. Keeping the heel deep and the lower leg slightly forwards increases security and prevents the rider from being thrown forwards and unseated if the horse does succeed.

Horses who buck out of exuberance or freshness can be lunged before riding to give them a chance to work off high spirits safely and settle down. They should also be turned out as often as possible, and the concentrate ration may need adjusting if it is excessive for the work done.

REARING

Rearing is one of the most dangerous vices a horse may have; it can be difficult to remedy and in many cases there is no guaranteed 'cure' as such. It is certainly not something which novice or inexperienced riders should try to deal with themselves; experienced and very competent help should be sought.

There are numerous reasons why a horse may begin rearing: nappiness, stubbornness, laziness, too severe a bit, a rough or heavy-handed rider, physical pain, or being asked for too great a degree of collection too soon. If the cause is immediately and correctly identified and dealt with, nothing worse may happen and the situation never arise again. Once rearing has become an established vice, however, the horse will always be a liability and it may be best to consider having him destroyed unless the problem is due to either the rider or physical pain of some kind; only an experienced person can help to decide this.

If for some reason a horse does threaten to rear, it may be possible to nip it in the bud by circling tightly with the inside hand carried very low and using plenty of leg to maintain forward impulsion. If this moment is missed and the horse does actually rear, it is vital that the rider stays well forward, placing the arms around the neck if possible and taking great care not to pull on the reins, which will result in loss of balance and the horse possibly falling. If the horse rears up very high there is a danger that he may topple over and come down on top of the rider; some horses will even do this intentionally. If this situation does arise, the rider should kick both feet free of the stirrups and slip off to the side, which requires quick thinking and quicker reactions.

If a horse rears, stay well forward and do not pull back on the reins in case he overbalances. If necessary, be prepared to slip your feet from the stirrups and slide off.

Sharp teeth can be a cause of bit evasions. They should be checked every six months by your vet and rasped if necessary.

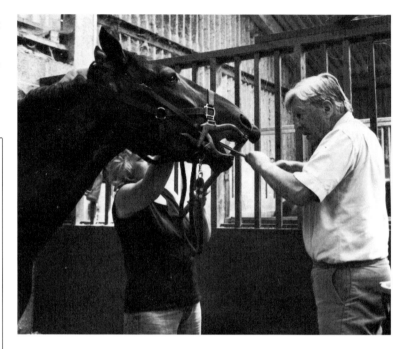

Types of Bit
While most horses are quite happy in metal bits provided they have been correctly trained and are properly ridden, there are always exceptions, and some do go better in rubber-covered, vulcanite or synthetic mouthpieces. An even smaller proportion dislike conventional bits of any description, in which case a bitless bridle may offer a satisfactory answer. They are potentially very severe however, so should definitely not be looked upon as being a 'soft' alternative to bitting.

There are a number of ways in which a horse may evade the action of the bit; rather than simply treating the symptoms, however, it is important to look deeper and try to remedy the root cause. If the horse is suffering from physical discomfort, for example – often the reason why evasions start in the first place – then it is obviously unfair to ignore it and simply strap his mouth shut with a noseband, and continue; even worse problems could even occur as a result of doing so.

More often than not the rider's hands themselves are to blame, although most prefer to blame previous owners, the type of bit – or

Mouth Ailments
Physical problems in the mouth such as sharp teeth, lampas and ulcers can cause bit evasions. It should not be forgotten that the horse's teeth do not wear evenly, and sharp edges will occur on the molar teeth, which should be checked every six months by the vet and rasped if necessary.

Grakle noseband.

Dropped noseband.

Rope noseband.

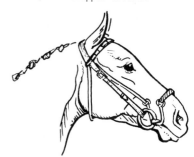

Kineton or puckle noseband.

anything except themselves! An independent, secure and balanced position is the only way in which to acquire 'good hands', but sadly, far too few people are prepared to put in the time and effort necessary to achieve this.

Ill-fitting tack can be another cause – not just a worn, over-large, too small or incorrectly adjusted bit, but a bridle which digs into the base of the ears or has too tight a throatlash; even a pinching saddle may be the source of the problem, causing the horse to hollow, run and come above the bit.

Once a horse has learnt a bit evasion it may continue, even after the source of the problem has been remedied, and it may be necessary to use a noseband designed to prevent it.

If it is felt that a different type of bit would be beneficial, some experimentation may be necessary. Buying a number of bits can be expensive, and it isn't always possible to borrow from friends. One solution is to hire a bit instead; many saddlers offer this service nowadays, and there are also bit hire services around the country which advertise in horse magazines.

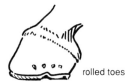

rolled toes

feather edged shoe

Rolled toes can be helpful with horses that tend to forge, overreach or drag their toes. Feather-edged shoes can reduce the danger of more serious injury to horses that brush badly.

Interfering is a general term used to cover various self-inflicted injuries caused by a hoof striking against or into, another leg. There can be a number of reasons why this may happen, including poor conformation, weakness, fatigue, lack of balance and suppleness, bad riding or poor shoeing – or a combination of any of these factors.

Whether a horse is prone to interfering or not, it is only sensible to protect your investment by using protective boots of some kind when riding. Riding lateral movements, lungeing, participating in cross-country work or exercising on non-level going are times when the risk of such injuries occurring will be increased. A bad knock or cut can mean a lengthy lay-off, usually when you least want it. Any boots which are used should be kept scrupulously clean to prevent chafing.

In some cases it can be useful to consult a farrier, who may suggest using shoes which will help minimize any injuries inflicted, or to help improve the gait. An eye should be kept on the state of the shoes as a matter of good management; a risen clench, for example, can cause a tremendous amount of damage.

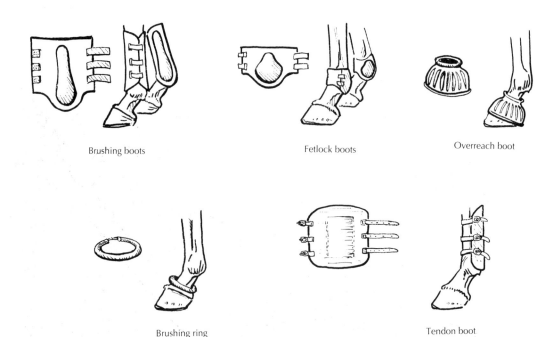

Brushing boots

Fetlock boots

Overreach boot

Brushing ring

Tendon boot

Like people, some horses are more naturally and conformationally predisposed than others to be athletic; however, with correct diet and training, a great deal can often be done to remedy this situation.

Clumsiness is frequently due to weakness – a lack of muscular development and suppleness – but since horses are fairly large animals, it can be all too easy to assume a strength and capacity for work which is not necessarily present. A horse that is young or unfit will not only be weak, but will also tire easily and quickly, so work should always be kept within his ability.

When schooling, use can be made of exercises (such as pole work) designed to supple, strengthen and improve co-ordination. This sort of work also serves to sharpen the concentration, lack of which can be a factor in clumsiness. Exercises involving turns, circles and transitions are also of benefit, since they will improve balance and increase motivation; the rider should try to obtain a regular rhythm and length of stride suitable to the size, ability and conformation of the horse.

Clumsiness can also be due to sloppy riding, age, poor shoeing, or some kind of physical problem or nervous disorder, so these possibilities should be investigated thoroughly.

Exercises such as pole work, aimed at improving strength, co-ordination, concentration, balance and suppleness will help improve clumsy horses.

Like clumsiness, stumbling may be due to lack of suppleness, strength or schooling, poor shoeing, inactivity, unbalanced riding, insufficient food or tiredness – or any of these in combination.

The horse may not be paying sufficient attention to where he is putting his feet, either through spooking at an object, lack of concentration or because he is disobeying the rider. There may also be physical problems such as arthritis. Low grade lameness may not be glaringly obvious to a lay person, but can be the reason for otherwise unexplained stumbling or general unsteadiness in the gaits, and a veterinary opinion should be sought.

Stumbling may also occur because of a stone lodged in the foot, or even if the horse is being ridden on particularly stony ground, especially if he has thin or flat soles; with the latter problem, shoeing with pads may help. Poor going – uneven, deep or rutted – should be avoided where possible, and when it is necessary to ride across it, the gait should be kept steady, active and balanced.

Horses with a tendency to stumble may benefit from being shod with rolled toes; knee boots should be used when hacking out along roads and hard surfaces likely to cause serious damage to the knee joints if the horse does fall.

Hoof Picks
It is a good idea to take along a hoof pick when hacking out, as a stone wedged into the hoof can be extremely difficult or even impossible to remove with fingers alone! The folding variety is absolutely ideal, since they fit easily into a pocket and have no protruding parts to cause injuries should you fall off.

 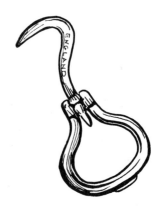

A folding hoofpick can be handy when out hacking, and is small enough to be easily slipped into a pocket.

Some horses can become highly excitable when being ridden, particularly more highly strung, temperamental types; with this sort of animal, a good daily routine, sympathetic handling and a sensible concentrate to exercise ratio is essential. Sensitivity and tactful riding is also likely to be called for.

Certain situations may cause excitable behaviour; for example, hunting, cantering while out hacking with other horses, any fast work, or the atmosphere on a show ground. The problem will be aggravated if the rider becomes tense or over-anxious, so this type of horse is not usually particularly suited to a novice, or an inexperienced or nervous person, who is unlikely to be able to provide the right combination of firmness and calm.

Horses that become excited when in the presence of others will benefit from working regularly in such conditions, as well as being turned out with other equines.

Turning horses out regularly in the company of others ultimately makes horses more relaxed and content, and reduces behavioural problems.

Canter seems to be the gait which presents most problems for the majority of riders, but with good riding and the application of a little thought, it should be possible to overcome most difficulties in time.

In most instances, spending a lot of time in the gait is not necessary; quality of gait is more important than quantity. As the trouble is resolved, and the horse becomes more established in the correct way of going, the rider becomes more confident, so it is an easy matter gradually to extend the period of time.

Often difficulties arise because the rider, having experienced a particular problem once, anticipates it happening again, and instead of dealing with it calmly and logically, panics a little, allowing the aids to become abrupt and the posture unbalanced.

With horses which are reluctant to move off accurately into canter, it is most often simply a matter of asking the horse to work with more impulsion and activity in the preceding gait, and to be more obedient to the leg aids. Although it may feel as though you are doing the wrong thing, it is also important to maintain a firm rein contact; allowing it to become slack will lead to loss of balance and the horse running on in an increasingly faster trot before he finally falls into an unbalanced canter. Use half-halts to help rebalance and reactivate the horse as a preparation to giving the aid to canter, and try to avoid tipping forwards; rather, think more in terms of almost bringing the upper body slightly behind the vertical.

Correct sequence of movement in canter – right foreleg leading.

Achieving the correct canter lead is another problem which can cause headaches for some riders. Stiffness can be a cause. A physical problem of some kind may also be responsible, and if the problem is consistent, a vet should be asked to check the horse over. Assuming this can be eliminated, first make sure that the aids for canter are correct and consistently the same so that the horse is not confused by the rider's request. If difficulties still arise, try riding an accurate 20m/yd diameter circle in walk, and then commencing the trot on a 10m/yd diameter circle towards the centre of the larger circle. On starting to trot, maintain the contact on both reins, and gently but firmly lift the inside rein upwards (not backwards) about 10–15cm (4–6in). When half-way round the smaller circle, maintain the position of the inside hand and ask for canter, returning to the 20m/yd circle at the same point as it was left. Having obtained the correct canter lead, keep the inside hand higher than the outside and continue cantering for one or two 20m/yd circles before smoothly returning to the trot and walk and praising the horse. After four or five days, when the correct canter lead can be consistently established, the rider can gradually begin to lower the inside hand until a normal position is achieved.

Horses may become 'disunited' in canter – that is, with the front legs in left canter and the hind legs in right canter, or vice versa – for a number of reasons: they may be asked to move too deeply through a corner, to turn too tightly, or the rider may give an abrupt rein aid or suddenly shift his weight, causing a loss of balance which the horse attempts to compensate for as well as he is able.

If the horse strikes off on to the wrong canter lead, or becomes disunited, return to the trot or walk, settle and reorganize yourselves and then ask again, so that incorrect and unbalanced cantering does not become a habit.

Cantering is good fun, especially when in company, but remember that horses can become over-excited when cantering together so take care not to allow things to get out of control.

The fact that shying is a natural reaction to an object that the horse perceives as being frightening or threatening does not reduce the fact that it is a dangerous habit at any time, and especially so when riding on the roads.

One possible cause which should certainly be looked into is poor or impaired vision, particularly if shying is a frequent occurrence. If the problem is over-freshness, fewer concentrates, more exercise and freedom out at grass may provide a satisfactory solution; the value of spending more time both schooling and handling the horse should not be overlooked either, particularly with more nervous and timid types. This will instil increased obedience as well as developing a better rapport, so the horse may feel able to place sufficient trust in the rider to overcome any genuine anxieties he may have.

Horses will often shy at what to us may seem perfectly normal, everyday objects as well as at things you might expect them to be startled by, so it is important to remain alert at all times when riding. Once a horse has shied at something in a particular place he may

Shying is a natural reaction to objects the horse perceives as being frightening or threatening. Where specific objects are known to cause problems – such as tractors, bin bags, road cones and so on – a programme of quiet and patient schooling near such things can help build confidence.

well shy there again every time thereafter, remembering the fright he had there previously – even though whatever startled him may no longer be there! Irritating though it may be, it is at least possible to anticipate the problem, and to take suitable action, such as waiting for traffic to overtake before asking him to walk past the trouble area. Most horses will attempt to keep as much distance as possible between themselves and the object of their anxiety, swinging their quarters away from it and trying to keep their heads turned towards it to keep it clearly in sight. The steps will become shorter and hesitant, and given the opportunity, the horse may attempt to swing round and move off briskly in the direction he came from.

The rider should try not to tense up, as this will only confirm the horse's idea that there is something to be frightened of, but, using a soothing voice and positive (not aggressive) riding, ask the horse to move forward, providing the road is clear. Turn the horse's head slightly away from the source of the problem and use plenty of leg on the inside of the bend achieved to help prevent the quarters from swinging away from it, and keep the horse moving in the desired direction; teaching movements such as leg-yielding and shoulder-in at home will help considerably in achieving this. Some horses may be better for being allowed to stop and take a good look at the object, consenting to walk forwards afterwards obediently if warily.

Great care does need to be exercised in dealing with this problem when on the roads; if the horse succeeds in spinning around, or exhibits a marked anxiety about passing an object he perceives as being frightening or threatening, the rider should halt him and re-gain control, waiting until the road is clear of vehicles before proceeding again. Roads aren't really the best places to indulge in sorting out shying problems because of the dangers involved, hence the importance of appropriate schooling at home.

Young Horses

Young, inexperienced horses are highly likely to spook at un-accustomed objects until they realize there is nothing to fear. Until greater confidence is developed, it is only sensible to ride out in company, preferably with a wiser, steadier, older horse as escort who can provide a good example as well as offering reassurance. Where the width of roads and visibility permits, it is often a good idea to ride abreast, keeping the escort horse between the youngster and passing traffic, where it will not only form a barrier, but also encourage motorists to keep to a steady speed.

Horses that are traffic shy are a danger not just to themselves but to their riders, passing motorists and pedestrians. One that has been badly frightened in the past may be impossible to ride out safely on the roads and should be worked only in a safe environment away from traffic.

Some may gain in confidence by hacking out along quiet lanes with a steady horse as escort riding abreast, forming a barrier between him and passing vehicles as well as encouraging motorists to slow down. Grazing a horse in a well-fenced field next to a busy road may also help a little, although there is no guarantee that either of these solutions will work or make the horse reliable to ride out unaccompanied.

Often it is particular types of vehicle which pose the problems – large lorries, buses, tractors, motorcycles or even pushbikes – and with careful, patient training and the help of drivers of the 'problem' vehicle, it may be possible to overcome his fears off the road in a safe environment such as a large field. Some riding clubs do hold 'traffic training' days where a selection of different motorized hazards and professional, experienced help are available, which can prove very helpful and successful.

Motorists

Whenever possible, do try to acknowledge courtesy shown by passing motorists when on the roads; a nod of the head will suffice if it is not advisable to take one hand from the reins.

Road Safety

Before riding out, do tell someone of your intended route (and stick to it!) and roughly how long you will be. Be prepared for an emergency by taking with you money for phone calls, and a pocket first aid kit, and carrying a piece of paper in your pocket with your name and a contact telephone number written on it, plus any medical conditions you have or drugs that you take. Wear fluorescent and reflective garments and avoid riding in conditions of poor visibility.

It is frequently necessary nowadays to cross or ride along busy roads to reach bridle-paths, but care should always be taken. Riders and horses should be wearing high-visibility garments which make it far easier for motorists to spot them at a distance.

Hacking should be a relaxing and enjoyable activity for horse and rider; if, however, the horse persists in continually jogging it becomes not only tiring, irritating and uncomfortable for both, but may eventually damage the horse's front limbs since it can result in excessive concussion.

When riding a horse inclined to jog, it is all too easy to become irritated and to reprimand it rather sharply with the bit, but this should be avoided, as should sustaining a continuous pull on the reins.

Jogging may arise as a result of too many concentrates and too little exercise; ensuring a more suitable work to food ratio, adopting a lower energy diet and ensuring that some time out at grass is allotted each day, is usually the answer in this situation.

More highly strung and temperamental horses may also be inclined to jog, as may very fit horses feeling extremely well and full of themselves – particularly on first coming out of the stable during the winter when they are clipped and the weather is chilly. It sometimes helps to settle the horse before hacking if time can be set aside to lunge or school for fifteen to twenty minutes beforehand.

Jogging can often also be a sign of discomfort, due to back pain, an ill-fitting saddle, or insensitive or rough riding. Gripping up with the lower leg or a poor position will cause the horse to increase his speed, and if the rider then tries to contain this by adopting a restrictive rein contact rather than by improving the posture or softening the leg aids, the result is a jolting jog trot. Trying to correct the horse with a strong contact can also lead to other problems such as coming above the bit to evade contact, over-bending, leaning on the rider's hands, and snatching at the bit, amongst others. Much patience will be needed to remedy the problem, using a soothing voice if the horse breaks into a jog, applying frequent gentle half-halts, and spending some time schooling to teach the horse to relax and accept the hand and leg.

When riding in company, it is usually best to place more excitable horses at the front where they will be more inclined to relax and settle; this is also a sensible policy to follow especially when cantering in groups. It does of course help if other riders are considerate of those experiencing problems, and avoid riding too hard on the heels of a horse in front, which can not only provoke jogging, but may also instigate a kick in response.

Small ponies may find it difficult to keep up with longer striding horses; the bigger animal should be slowed, rather than the smaller one pushed on. If he is hurried too fast, it will result in his becoming unbalanced and breaking into a jog.

Nappiness – refusing to obey the rider's aids – may arise for a number of reasons, including stubbornness and bad temper, fatigue, unwillingness to leave home, or groups of other horses, and asking the horse to do something he cannot cope with.

A nappy horse will remain rooted to the spot, ignoring the rider's aids to move in any direction but the one he chooses – usually back towards home. If the rider insists, he may show signs of temper and exhibit dangerous habits such as running backwards or rearing.

Nappiness often starts in youth: demanding too much too soon, confusion as to what is being asked, or poor training may all lead to mutiny if the horse feels psychologically over-stretched, insecure, anxious or tired. Discomfort from physical causes or ill-fitting tack may also cause the horse to look for ways of avoiding work.

Nervous or inexperienced riders can also contribute to, or cause, the problem; horses are not machines and may occasionally play up. If the rider does not cope satisfactorily and competently when this happens, minor misdemeanours can escalate and become more serious, since, having been successful once or twice in getting his own way, the horse repeats it. Horses can also become set in their ways. If the rider always follows a particular routine – whether riding for a certain length of time each day, always following the same route when hacking, or even just going to a particular point and then doubling back on his tracks – the horse can become

Napping.

resentful and resistant if the rider asks him to continue for longer, or to go in a different direction.

There is no single perfect cure for nappiness once the habit has become established, and such horses may never be suitable for novice riders, as, although the problem can be corrected to an extent, the tendency will still remain and can resurface. It is best if any signs of nappiness are nipped in the bud the instant they are exhibited, with firm, positive riding. The better schooled and more obedient the horse is the less likely such problems are to arise, and the easier it will be to correct if they do.

At the first sign of hesitation, the rider should send the horse positively forward, using seat, legs, voice and, if necessary and safe to do so, the stick; adopting a position with the upper body which is slightly behind the movement is helpful.

If the horse succeeds in stopping and the rider can not re-initiate forward movement, circle tightly, provided it is safe, keeping the inside hand low and using plenty of inside leg to create movement. After a few circles send the horse on again; if he still refuses to do so, repeat the circling exercise again until he does move in the desired direction. Although it may take some time, this method does eventually work. When out on the roads with a horse known to be nappy, it is advisable to have an assistant follow on foot or bicycle to help control traffic if difficulties arise.

The instant the horse begins to show signs of resistance he must be ridden forwards strongly.

Water fences are a popular feature on both cross-country courses and pleasure rides, but many people have problems at such obstacles; usually, it has to be said, because of lack of preparation.

Those lucky enough to live in coastal regions where riding is permitted along the beach have an ideal training ground, as the horse can be worked along the edge of the water while the tide is out, gradually building up to splashing through the shallows. Others are not so lucky, but to overcome a horse's fears a suitable area of water needs to be found. Ideally this should have a firm bottom giving good footing, and should graduate from very shallow to slightly deeper; the clearer the water the better, as the horse will gain confidence from this. If you have a stream nearby this could be ideal provided it meets such criteria, but do check the bottom in waders or wellington boots first, in case there are hidden pot-holes or concealed rubbish, and do not attempt to enter it where the banks are very steep and slippery. If the horse becomes frightened, you may be able to bully him in once, but may never succeed again! If suitable streams are unavailable, hire the facilities of a local cross-country course.

Do not overlook any opportunity for riding through water, however mundane! Starting with shallow puddles may in fact make it easier to tackle wider or deeper expanses later on.

If possible, take along a friend with an experienced horse who can offer a lead; although walking in leading your horse may convince him that it is safe to walk in, he is more likely to trust and follow the example set by another equine. Ride quietly but positively forwards to the shallow end – using speed is only likely to lead to a ducking for you! Urge the horse forward with legs and voice and a tap from the stick if necessary; but do not resort to bullying tactics. Much time and patience may be necessary. Offering a titbit as an inducement may help; once the horse begins to move forwards, be quick to follow up your advantage and send him on into the water then you can halt and praise him. Be careful if he starts to paw at the water, as it may be a sign that he is going to roll; if this happens keep a firm contact on the reins and walk forwards again. Having been in once, it will be easier the second time, and once he is happy with the sensation of water splashing around his legs and under his belly you can try trotting into and out of the water. Always approach water steadily, with impulsion, not speed, otherwise the drag of the water can bring the horse down.

Do not overlook other opportunities for introducing horses to water, such as hosing the feet and legs, and walking through large puddles or flooded sections of roads in rainy weather.

Any horse that participates in cross-country events must be comfortable with water jumps.

Of all jumping problems, this one must be the commonest! There can be a number of reasons for horses to do this, including:

1. Fences too high or too wide. Even though a horse may have popped over one or two bigger fences, continually asking him to jump at the extreme limit, or beyond his ability, will soon frighten him.

Refusals can happen for a number of reasons, including asking the horse to jump a fence beyond his ability.

2. Unfamiliarity with a type of fence. Lack of experience may cause a horse to refuse if he meets a strange obstacle he has not seen before. Schooling at home over obstacles with plenty of variety, and including known 'bogey' fences at very low heights soon increases confidence and boldness.

3. Ill-fitting tack. Too strong a bit, particularly if the rider is rather heavy handed, can lead to stops. When riding strong horses it may be necessary to experiment with different bits until a compromise is reached, whereby the rider can safely remain in control, without making the horse frightened or anxious. Pain from a badly fitting saddle can also cause refusals.

4. A poor approach. Asking the horse to take off too far away from a fence (or too close), riding in an unbalanced way, lacking in impulsion, or approaching at a very acute angle, will all cause problems. If the horse is continually badly presented to a fence he will soon lose confidence, and refusals will happen regularly.

5. Physical problems. Physical pain may be a cause; do not overlook the possibility of poor eyesight being to blame either, but ask the vet to check on this too.

6. Bad going. Very hard ground can cause jarring and soreness, particularly to the front legs, resulting in a shortened, choppy stride and a reluctance to jump fluently, if at all. Very deep or slippery going may also cause a lack of confidence.

Slippery ground can affect a horse's confidence and cause him to refuse; fitting studs to offer better purchase may help.

7. Poor or dazzling light. Jumping from light to dark or from dark to well-lit areas may cause problems, and when approaching such fences, it is best to adopt a steady approach so as to give the horse's vision as much time as possible to adjust. Newly painted fences in bright light may also dazzle momentarily.

8. Tiredness. Try to finish earlier on a good effort, rather than being tempted to carry on a little longer; a tired horse will become rebellious and disobedient.

9. Nappiness and disobedience. *See* page 70.

10. Poor rider position. Repeatedly getting left behind, or restricting the horse with the reins, can often be responsible for refusals; no matter how good the horse, he will not carry on forever if this continually happens.

11. Sourness. Doing an excessive amount of jumping can start to cause refusals. Avoid over-schooling over fences, and be

selective about competitions and classes; do not try to do too many or too often, particularly when the ground is hard during the summer. Horses that have become sour will benefit from a break, and when they return to jumping work may regain their zest by doing some hunting or cross-country work.

Sometimes the reason for refusing can be quite obvious and understandable, but if the causes listed above can be satisfactorily eliminated, it may be necessary to ask whether it is not so much a case of the horse stopping, as the rider. If the rider is a little anxious for some reason, he may subconsciously not really want to jump the fence. Although he may go through the motions of riding vigorously, he will be a little half-hearted, which soon communicates itself to the horse.

Particularly when it comes to tackling larger fences, some riders are not always as bold and fearless as they like to imagine, even though the fences themselves may be well within the horse's scope. It is important in this case to be honest, to appreciate any limitations before the horse's confidence becomes completely ruined, and to go back to smaller fences and competitions for a while. Seeking the help of an experienced instructor to improve position and to begin to develop an eye for a stride is often invaluable.

AFTER A REFUSAL

After a refusal many riders make the mistake of approaching the fence again at great speed, and not always with a lot of co-ordination; if the horse was not over-worried about jumping previously, he soon will be if ridden like this, lacking balance, impulsion and time to judge and adjust his stride for a correct take-off. Although the rider may feel that he is taking charge of the situation, he is not really in control, and if the horse does stop again, it will be far more unseating.

A refusal can shake both the horse's and rider's nerve, so be prepared to lower the fence if necessary, get the horse going forward again between hand and leg and reapproach with impulsion at a controlled pace, not at speed. If the horse begins to prop or falter, the rider will then have plenty of time to take action, closing the legs and pushing the horse forward into the contact. Once confidence has been restored, the fence can be rebuilt again in gradual stages.

Using the Whip
Never hold a horse in front of a fence and give him a smack with the whip for refusing – or give him a smack and restrict him with your hands from going forwards, as this can lead to the horse trying to jump from a standstill or rearing. If it is felt that a smack is justified in the circumstances, turn the horse away from the fence before doing so, and allow him to move briskly forwards before gently steadying him; do not contradict yourself by effectually telling him to go forward and stop at the same time.

Running out can happen for similar reasons as refusing – pain, a poor approach, asking the horse to jump a fence too big or too wide for his ability, or through the rider being half-hearted.

Very often the rider will have suddenly dropped or pushed his hands forwards on the last part of the approach, and/or anticipated the fence and tipped forwards. This loss of initiative not only gives the horse the opportunity to run out, but unbalances him on his forehand, so it would be difficult for him to tackle the fence anyway.

While it is possible to lean poles against the front of the fence to form a channel, this sort of assistance is not available at shows, so it is not ideal to rely on it at home. It is far better to go back a few steps and rebuild confidence and control jumping smaller fences. Approach straight, with impulsion (not speed) and from a slower gait such as trot, rather than canter, if necessary. Check that the upper body is vertical or even very slightly behind the vertical to help keep the horse moving forward and straight from the leg into the contact; although this should not mean that you get left behind.

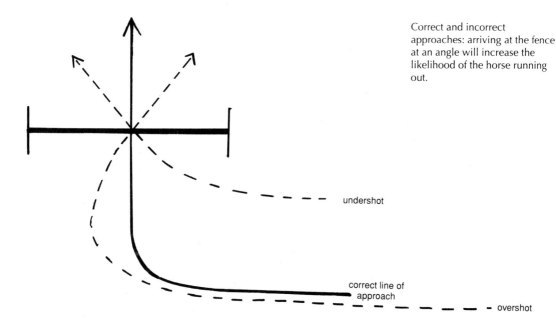

Correct and incorrect approaches: arriving at the fence at an angle will increase the likelihood of the horse running out.

undershot

correct line of approach

overshot

Most people assume that a horse that jumps at speed must be enjoying it, yet very often the reverse is true. Frequently the horse lacks confidence or is frightened, and is trying to get the job over and done with as quickly as possible. Jumping in this manner may not only be alarming for the rider, but can eventually end in mishap, because of inaccurate approaches, careless jumping, or lack of balance between fences, particularly on turns.

Try to work out why the horse is worried; it may stem from physical pain or ill-fitting saddlery, causing the horse to try to run away from the source of discomfort. The rider getting left behind, restricting the headcarriage or jabbing on the contact, can also upset and panic the horse. Sometimes the rider can be responsible in other ways for creating the problem; if there have been problems in the past with refusing, for example, the rider may be so anxious to prevent it from happening again that he rides the horse forward over strongly and too fast, so the horse becomes quicker and quicker. The rider assumes he has done the right thing, but the horse is in fact progressively losing confidence rather than having it restored.

Rushing will also happen if the horse's flat work is lacking; to ride correctly to fences, he must accept, and be obedient to, both hand and leg. Spend more time concentrating on this aspect of schooling,

Controlling Frustration
When schooling or re-training a horse patience is vital, but can sometimes be in short supply. If you find yourself becoming exasperated or frustrated by a horse you are working on, quite often the best thing you can do is either to put him away or to go for a quiet hack instead, so you can both cool off. This will also give you more time for thought, so that on returning to the problem later on refreshed in mind and body, you may have thought up a more successful way of approaching it!

Rushing is most frequently due to fear and lack of confidence; it may be necessary to return to basics, concentrating on flat work and pole work before gradually reintroducing small fences.

perhaps combining it with work over poles. As the flat work and pole work improves, so fences can be introduced, keeping them small and simple initially so that both horse and rider are more inclined to be relaxed and confident. Incorporating jumping exercises into flat work sessions can be a useful way of helping to settle a more highly strung animal, and encouraging him to treat jumping in a more workmanlike manner.

Exercises such as circling both before and after fences can sometimes be helpful. Also, building more varied and boldly painted obstacles will often encourage the horse to slow down a little on the approach so he can take a better look. With naturally very sharp horses, the rider must maintain impulsion, but should otherwise concentrate on sitting very quietly on the approach; resist the temptation either to chase him on the last few strides, or to have a very strong backwards tension on the reins which can encourage the horse to run on even more.

Should the horse become anxious and hurried, be patient and take care not to over-correct him. Whether schooling on the flat or over fences, severe reprimands via the bit are always to be avoided unless circumstances make it imperative for the safety of horse and rider that he slows or stops as quickly as possible.

Jumping at speed tends to be unsafe or inaccurate; this horse has hollowed and is trailing his legs as a result.

Young horses will sometimes snake a little on the approach to fences through greenness. Where this happens with older horses, however, it is usually because they tend to rush or are gassy in the first place, and the rider attempts to exert control largely with the reins and insufficient leg. The more the rider tries to use his hands incorrectly to position the horse the worse it tends to become. The problem can also arise through a poor approach, over- or under-shooting the turn to the fence.

As with so many jumping problems, going back to basics is the answer, teaching the horse to accept and work correctly between hand and leg, schooling him to move away from the pressure of each leg as well as to go forwards quietly from it, and practising riding school movements accurately. In the case of a horse who tends to rush (which can encourage the rider to become over-strong with his hands and reluctant to keep his legs in contact), this approach has benefits, but the initial cause of the rushing should also be investigated fully.

Correcting any deviation from a straight approach will become easier as the flat work improves. If the horse begins to dive to one side, use more leg on that side to straighten him and keep a definite

Rein Contact
Try to avoid using the rein contact to prevent the horse drifting, as it can cause it to begin hollowing in the air, or even to start to refuse.

An inaccurate turn to a fence will result in a crooked approach. This rider needs to sit straighter, use more outside leg and hand, and plan her approaches more carefully.

Poles can be used in a variety of ways to encourage a horse to remain straight over fences. If using a 'V' of poles as here, do not close the point of the 'V' up too much.

contact to that rein. If the rider pulls on the opposite one instead, it will only have the effect of restricting forward movement on that side, and make the horse frustrated and more inclined to crab sideways; the more level the contact can be made and with as little bend in the neck, the better.

Drifting to one side in the air over a fence is often caused by the rider either keeping an over-strong contact on one rein, or by folding forwards to one side – especially if he is anticipating making a turn in a particular direction on landing.

Leaning a pole diagonally across the front of a fence and using verticals and spreads of cross poles will help encourage the horse to remain straight in the air. If the horse consistently drifts in one particular direction, building the fence up higher on that side will also help.

Improving the flat work is also helpful; by teaching the horse to move away from the pressure of one stronger leg, it will be possible to correct any drifting by use of the leg on that side.

Physical problems may be a cause and should not be overlooked; if the rider can be eliminated as being blameless, it is worth asking a vet to check out all possibilities, including teeth, back, feet and legs, and even vision.

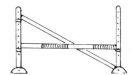

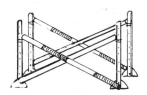

Poles may be used in a variety of ways when schooling to encourage straightness across a fence.

Meeting an unfamiliar fence can cause a horse to be spooky and wary of it, often jumping higher than necessary to clear it. This can be a frightening experience in itself for the horse, particularly if the rider is caught unawares and gets left behind.

Horses that tend to be 'spooky' when jumping – approaching fences very cautiously – are not necessarily 'problem' horses. In fact they often prove to be the best showjumpers in the long term, as they are naturally very careful, concentrating on the fence, and often jumping a little bit bigger than necessary in order to avoid touching it.

It is very important with this sort of horse not to try to rush or bully him, otherwise you can rapidly destroy his confidence and he may begin to refuse or run out. Youngsters especially may be rather spooky when first learning to jump, as it is a whole new experience to them, and they may be uncertain at first about how to proceed. Rather than increasing the height or width of a fence, try instead to broaden the horse's experience by building as many different types of obstacle as possible, introducing variety in the form of filler boards, planks, gates, walls, and by freshening up old jump equipment with a lick of new paint. Until the horse is going forwards more boldly, and tackling strange obstacles with confidence, keep them very small so they can be easily popped over from a trot if necessary. The rider must make sure that he stays in a good balance, not interfering or restricting with the rein contact in the air, or doing anything else which might upset or worry the horse.

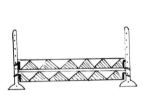

Many different types of fence can be introduced to broaden a young or green horse's experience, but keep them very low initially until he is more confident.

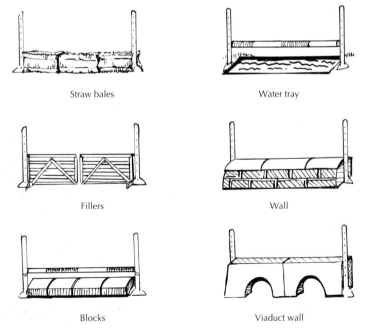

Straw bales

Water tray

Fillers

Wall

Blocks

Viaduct wall

Some horses are naturally more careful than others; either a horse is careful or he is not, and not much can be done to change the fact. While most horses do not like hitting fences, using very heavy poles to try to teach him to be more careful will only frighten him, and may lead to injury.

If the horse tends to have fences down because he lacks a good style – failing to tuck his front legs up tightly for instance – it may well be worth while introducing some schooling exercises using placing poles and grids of fences to try to improve it. Lack of athleticism over jumps may also be due to insufficient good basic schooling on the flat; working on this aspect can only be beneficial and will certainly make any jumping exercises more successful.

Although a horse may be very careful and tidy when being jumped at home, he will sometimes have fences down when competing at shows, often because of rider nerves. Very often the fence which is knocked down is either the first, the last, or one the rider is a little apprehensive about. Consequently the rider may try to approach too carefully or too aggressively, trying hard but actually riding less well and upsetting or mispresenting the horse. It is easy for the pressure of competition and the desire to do well to affect your riding adversely, but the more experience you get, the more you will be able to relax and, often, the better the results will be.

Complacency, boredom, rushing, lack of concentration and insufficient impulsion can also be responsible for fences being knocked down. Fences should also be kept within the horse's scope: if they are too high or wide for his ability or stage of training, he will soon become frightened and worse problems may arise as a result.

Suffering from ring nerves can cause refusals at shows, but more experience will help. If necessary, stick at first to smaller classes which you know are well within both your own and your horse's capabilities; if the horse's winnings are such that he is ineligible for beginners and novice classes, you may still be able to compete 'hors concours' purely for the experience.

REFUSAL TO LOAD

Boots or Bandages?
With more excitable horses, protective boots with velcro fastenings are often preferable to bandages as they are quicker and easier to put on and take off. In addition, they do not need to be rolled up again after use ready for the next time, so are labour saving too!

Horses have extremely good memories, particularly for unpleasant or frightening experiences. It is not surprising then, if a horse that has had a bad journey or suffered rough, insensitive or even down-right brutal handling in the past is not keen to repeat it. Much time – weeks or possibly even months – may be needed to restore confidence. Sometimes a horse will become difficult to load because of its association with an event he does not particularly relish; trips to the vet, or to competitions. Even with a horse who is a willing loader and good traveller it does no harm to take him occasionally for a short trip, unload him and take him for a quiet, relaxing ride for a change, to dispel any such associations.

Care should always be taken to drive carefully and steadily, bearing in mind that the horse cannot anticipate acceleration, deceleration or corners. Some horses will always be happier travelling in a lorry than a trailer; not only do they offer more choice of travelling position, but tend to give a smoother ride.

When trying to teach a horse to load confidently, always use protective clothing, as injuries can arise as easily then as when

Dressed for travelling.

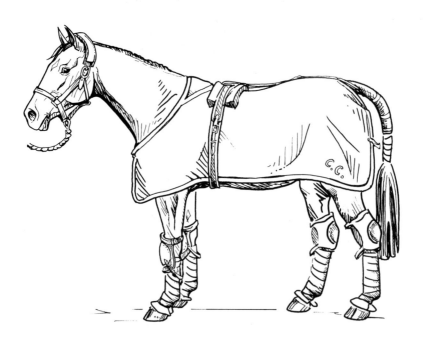

No matter how short a journey you are contemplating, or even if only practising loading, always put protective clothing on your horse.

Poll guard; this cap-type design is probably the best.

actually travelling. Both the handler and any assistants should wear hard hats, sensible footwear and gloves.

Youngsters

If you are dealing with a youngster, give him time to get used to the feel of protective boots or bandages long before attempting to load him, as you do not want to introduce too many exciting or worrying experiences all at once. The sensation of having these on will be strange to him at first, and he may lift his feet up very high. Take care when putting them on in case the horse panics or kicks out in alarm.

Young horses may not be intentionally awkward, but rather apprehensive, so be patient and allow them time to inspect the trailer or lorry.

A front-unload trailer is useful in encouraging unwilling loaders, as they can see daylight at the other end and will be less reluctant to enter. The handler should be wearing gloves and a hard hat for safety.

Claustrophobia

This can often play a part in loading difficulties: many more horses suffer from it than is perhaps realized. In severe cases it may not prove possible to travel the horse safely at all, although milder ones may be able to cope with short trips provided adequate space is allowed.

Here a horse-box has been used to form a barrier on one side of the trailer, while leaving the front ramp down and moving the partition across to give more room help make the trailer look less forbidding. Some bedding laid down and a more level site would have been ideal.

Horses are easily frightened if they feel the ramp moving as they place their hooves on it. Site the lorry or trailer on level ground, using a block or brick beneath the ramp if necessary to help steady it. With a trailer, lower the jockey wheel and trailer jacks even if it is still attached to the towing vehicle so that it feels more stable. Horses that have back problems may find steep ramps (often a problem with lorries) difficult to negotiate, and it may be necessary to find a bank or incline to lower the ramp on to make the gradient shallower.

Make the trailer or lorry look as inviting as possible, laying a little bedding down inside, and removing or tying back any internal partitions so as to create a spacious appearance, and to minimize the danger of the horse catching a hip on them. If you have a front-unload trailer leave the front ramp down so the horse can see daylight from the loading side.

The person leading the horse should walk beside his shoulder; getting in front of him will block his view and inhibit his desire to go forwards – and should he plunge forward the handler would be in great danger. A headcollar will not offer sufficient control with a fractious horse or one that is inclined to barge or plunge forwards, so a bridle should be substituted.

Never try to pull a reluctant horse forwards; doing so will only make him pull back more, or even attempt to rear. If he does run backwards try to go with him rather than get involved in a tug of war in which you will inevitably be the loser. Encourage the horse to move forwards by using food as an enticement; sometimes getting an assistant to lift each front foot in turn and place it on the ramp will encourage the horse to move forwards. However, care should be taken not to get in the way of the hooves when doing this.

If this does not prove successful, position the trailer or lorry alongside a wall or hedge to make positioning the horse on the ramp easier, and engage some competent assistants to encourage him forward from behind. A long-handled yard broom with stiff bristles pushed firmly up or scrubbed against the quarters is often enough persuasion. Anyone stationed behind the horse must be careful not to be in the line of fire in case the horse panics or retaliates by kicking out.

Another solution is to attach a lunge rein to one side of the trailer or lorry, so that, as the horse walks up to the ramp, the person holding the lunge rein walks behind, carefully bringing it round the quarters until he reaches the other side. It is then gradually shortened and tightened to apply pressure, pushing the horse up the

Ways of using lunge reins with one or two assistants to load a difficult horse.

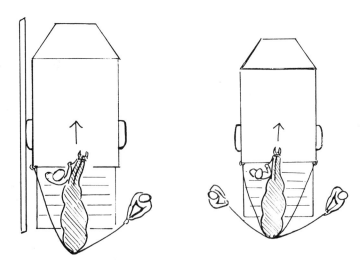

ramp. More effective still is to use two lunge reins, one on each side, and cross them behind the horse.

Once the horse is in the trailer or lorry, praise him and reward him with a titbit or two. With awkward horses it often helps to try to load them every day if possible, and even to feed them in the trailer or lorry rather than the stable.

BARGING IN/OUT OF VEHICLE

When dealing with horses that barge, do ensure that loading and unloading takes place in a safe environment; preferably enclosed in case the horse succeeds in escaping, and not close to barbed wire or hazards such as parked vehicles or machinery into which the horse might run. Avoid loading off surfaces which do not offer much purchase for metal-shod hooves, such as tarmac.

Horses which tend to barge should be led in a bridle rather than a headcollar, and a Chifney bit is excellent for this purpose. Remain by the horse's shoulder so that you do not get knocked down or trampled on, as well as retaining more control. Horses which barge may do so because of lack of obedience and training when being led generally; if so, this should be remedied before attempting to

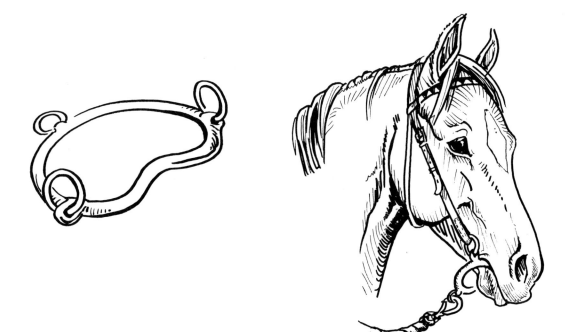

A Chifney bit.

load him. They may also do so through fear – perhaps they caught a hip on a doorway or against a partition previously. Make sure there are no projections, that partitions are removed or swung back and secured, and that the horse is led in a straight line up the ramp and into the interior.

Horses which shoot rapidly backwards out of a trailer when un-loading can be dissuaded from doing so by using a model with a front-unload ramp. The horse will then become accustomed to un-loading by walking forwards rather than backwards. When loading, always secure the breeching straps once the horse is inside before attempting to put up the ramp; this should be done standing to the side, never directly behind him. The breeching straps should be fitted at the correct height so that the horse cannot slide backwards under-neath them.

With a lorry this problem is far easier to deal with: arrange the partitions so the horse is standing sideways or diagonally at the front end, and have someone ready behind to swing the partition across to keep him enclosed.

Even though they may load and unload fairly happily and confidently, some horses are poor travellers once in motion, and scrabble, repeatedly losing their balance and even falling over. Especially in a trailer, a tendency to scrabble will do nothing to improve the horse's ride or increase his confidence. Whenever transporting horses, whether in a lorry or trailer, it must be remembered that they cannot anticipate acceleration, deceleration or cornering, so great care for the equine passengers must be taken. It can be quite an enlightening and educational experience for some so-called 'considerate' drivers to try standing in the horse's travelling area themselves (minus the horse) and to be driven around a field; this will certainly give some insight and understanding of the problems the horse faces.

Many people advocate narrow partitions to help 'prop up' poor travellers; in fact, this frequently aggravates the problem, creating the added danger that if the horse does fall down be may become wedged and unable to regain his feet. To balance properly, the horse must be able to spread all four legs, so ample provision needs to be made for this, rather than limiting the space available. In trailers, it may be found that the horse travels better without a central partition, although a breastbar should still be fitted. Others will only travel happily in a lorry, where you can experiment with different partition arrangements.

If you are unused to towing it is worth practising first with an empty trailer before attempting it with a horse on board; a large field is also an ideal place to learn how to manoeuvre!

Bit evasions Attempts to avoid contact with the bit. A horse that suffers discomfort in his mouth while being ridden due to physical problems such as sharp teeth, rough hands, or an ill-fitting or worn bit, may try to evade the contact. This may be exhibited in different ways, such as drawing the tongue back over the mouthpiece of the bit, opening his mouth, crossing his jaws, raising his head excessively high, leaning down onto the reins, snatching at them or attempting to run away.

Bolting (1) Eating food greedily and too rapidly resulting in poor digestion. (2) A horse running away with the rider in a blind panic.

Box-walking Refers to the habit of continually pacing around the stable; usually a nervous habit.

Brushing When the hoof of one foot strikes against the inside of the fetlock joint of the opposite one, through poor conformation, weakness, fatigue or bad shoeing.

Clipping Removing the coat, normally in the winter, in order to prevent excessive sweating and allow the horse to work harder without becoming distressed.

Clothing bib A broad flap fitted to lie just beneath the horse's lower jaw to prevent him from catching hold of and tearing, rugs and stable clothing.

Cold-backed Describes a horse that recoils, or reacts violently by bucking, plunging or throwing himself to the ground, when an attempt is made to saddle him.

Coprophagia Eating droppings.

Cow kick A forward-aimed kick from the back legs, which can be injurious to anyone standing by, or mounting, the horse.

Crib-biter A horse that grasps hold of a projection with his front teeth and then swallows air.

Cribox A proprietary substance with an unpleasant taste, used to apply to surfaces and objects to discourage chewing.

Gridwork A combination of obstacles set at specific distances from each other to help develop a better style of jumping.

Gymnastic jumping A form of jumping training using poles on the ground and/or combinations of fences set at specific distances from each other to encourage greater athleticism, boldness and quicker reactions in the horse.

Headshy Describes a horse that is nervous of having his head handled, and on whom it may be difficult to put a headcollar or bridle. It is usually due to the horse having been roughly handled.

Interfering A horse that knocks against one foot or leg with another.

Lungeing Training a horse to move on a large circle around the handler who maintains contact with a long rein, obeying vocal commands to halt, walk, trot or canter.

Mareishness   Excessive irritability exhibited by a mare in season.

Muzzle   A bucket-shaped object placed over the nose and held in place by a headpiece to prevent a horse from eating bedding or droppings, or tearing rugs.

Nappiness   Disobedience by the horse, who refuses to move forward or in the direction asked of him by the rider.

Quidding   Dropping partially chewed balls of food from the mouth; usually indicative of sharp teeth or some other mouth problem causing discomfort when chewing.

Rearing   The horse stands on his back legs, lifting his front legs up in the air.

Security marking   A method of marking horses in order to deter thieves and enable easy identification of strayed or stolen animals. Methods in the UK include permanent branding with super-chilled markers, inserting a microchip into the neck, and branding the hooves. Lip and ear tattooing are alternatives available in other countries.

Shy feeder   A horse with a poor appetite, who picks at his feeds.

Shying   An evasive action taken by a horse in order to avoid going near an object he is frightened of.

Sweet itch   An allergic reaction to the bite of a particular species of biting midge, *Culicoides*, resulting in extreme irritation and scratching of the affected areas along the crest of the neck, withers and base of the tail.

Tethering   A less than ideal method of restricting the movements of horses that are difficult to catch, or of utilizing unfenced pasture; a stout headcollar or padded neck collar is attached to a length of rope or chain which in turn is secured to a stake hammered into the ground.

Transition   Changing from one gait, or gait variant, to another.

Twitch   A wooden handle with a loop of cord threaded through a hole at one end, used to restrain a fractious horse for a specific purpose such as having its teeth rasped, or being clipped. The cord is passed over the upper lip and twisted until it is tight; this action is thought to cause the release of endorphins which sedate the horse.

Weaving   A horse who stands in his stable, swinging his head and neck, and swaying from side to side, sometimes quite violently.

Windsucking   The same as crib-biting, except that the horse does not need to grasp hold of an object with his front teeth in order to swallow air.

ASSOCIATIONS AND SOCIETIES

Association of British Riding Schools
Old Brewery Yard
Penzance
Cornwall TR18 2SL

British Equestrian Trade Association
Wothersome Grange
Bramham
Nr Wetherby
West Yorkshire LS23 6LY

British Horse Society
British Equestrian Centre
Stoneleigh
Kenilworth
Warwickshire CV8 2LR

Equine Behaviour Study Circle
Flat 2
169 Sumatra Road
West Hampstead
London NW6 1PE

or: Dr Sharon E Cregier
University of Prince Edward Island
Charlottetown
Prince Edward Island
Canada C1A 4P3

or: Mrs Sheree Cavaye
Lot 12
Singleton Road
Wilberforce
NSW 2756 Australia

National Equine Welfare Committee
c/o Bransby Home of Rest for Horses
Bransby
Nr Saxilby
Lincolnshire LN1 2PH

Riding for the Disabled Association
Avenue R
National Agricultural Centre
Stoneleigh
Kenilworth
Warwickshire CV8 2LY

Side Saddle Association
Highbury House
19 High Street
Welford
Northamptonshire NN6 7HT

Western Equestrian Society
Hillview Cottage
Windmill Lane
Ladbroke
Leamington Spa
Warwickshire CV33 0BN

Western Horseman's Society of Great Britain
13 East View
Barnet
Hertfordshire EN5 5TL

Worshipful Company of Farriers
37 The Uplands
Loughton
Essex IG10 1NQ

Worshipful Company of Saddlers
Saddlers' Hall
Gutter Lane
Cheapside
London EC2V 6BR

American Farriers Association
4089 Iron Works Pike
Lexington
KY 40511

American Horse Council
1700 K St., NW
Suite 300
Washington DC 20006

American Horse Protection Association
1000 29th Street, NW
#T-100
Washington DC 20007

American Horse Shows Association
220 E. 42nd Street
Suite 409
New York
NY 10017

American Riding Instructor Certification
Program
PO Box 4076
Mount Holly
NJ 08060

North American Riding for the Handicapped
Association
PO Box 33150
Denver
CO 80233

United States Pony Clubs
893 Matlock Street, #110
West Chester
PA 19382

PRODUCTS

Equisafe Tie Ring:
E.S.P.
Unit 1A
Mainline Business Centre
74 Station Road
Liss
Hampshire GU33 7AD

Identichip:
Animalcare Ltd
Common Road
Dunnington
York YO1 5RU

MMB Farmkey:
28 West Bar
Banbury
Oxfordshire OX16 9RR

Equibrand:
Church Street
Charwelton
Northamptonshire NN11 6YT

BHS in association with Threshold Books, *Transporting Horses by Road* (1986)

Britton, Vanessa, *Basic Tack*, The Crowood Press (1994)

Bush, Karen, *The Problem Horse*, The Crowood Press (1992)

Bush, Karen and Irving, Ross, *Successful Jumping – Training Your Horse with Gridwork*, The Crowood Press (1993)

Bush, Karen and Viccars, Sarah, *Solve Your Horse and Pony Problems*, Elliot Right Way Books (1992)

Drummond, Marcy, *Horse Management*, The Crowood Press (1991)

Hadley, Stephen, *Training the Showjumper*, Threshold Books (1987)

Harris, Charles, *Fundamentals of Riding*, J.A. Allen & Co Ltd (1985)

Kiley-Worthington, Dr Marthe, *The Behaviour of Horses*, J.A. Allen & Co Ltd

Larter, Chris and Jackman, Tony, *Transporting Your Horse or Pony*, David & Charles (1987)

McBane, Susan, *Behaviour Problems in Horses*, David & Charles; *Horse Tack*, David & Charles (1992)

Morris, Desmond, *Horse Watching*, Jonathan Cape (1988)

Rees, Lucy, *The Horse's Mind*

Thelwall, Jane, *The Less Than Perfect Horse*, Kingswood

Townley, Audrey, *Natural Riding*, The Crowood Press (1990); *The Natural Horse*, The Crowood Press (1993)

Williams, Moyra, *Horse Psychology*, J.A. Allen & Co; *Understanding Nervousness in Horses and Riders*, J.A. Allen & Co Ltd